The Complete Guide to Partnership Marketing

A step by step guide on creating successful marketing collaborations

James Cristal

ISBN: 1517515181
ISBN-13: 978-1517515188

CONTENTS

1. INTRODUCTION

Why Partnership Marketing?

Marketing as a subject comprises of everything from Digital Marketing to Out-of-Home Advertising, including models such as McCarthy's Marketing Mix and Porter's Five Forces. However, the idea of brand collaborations seems to have been lost within these theories and practices. Why is that? Is it because it is simply not a useful marketing technique?

It is fair to say that Partnership Marketing has been simply swept under the marketing rug. Read any marketing text book and you will find chapters on digital, social, strategy and branding, and amongst these you will notice the odd reference to brand synergies between two companies.

However, search online and you will find articles, agencies, and job adverts on Partnership Marketing all under an array of titles; Joint Marketing, Co-Marketing, and Merchant Marketing.

There are also thousands of global brands that participate in Partnership Marketing, from Virgin to Google, Pepsi to O2, and Apple to American Express. It is becoming clear then that it's an emerging subject, and after you read this book I am sure you will agree with my view that it should be acknowledged as one of the most important marketing techniques to materialise in recent times.

21st century technology has enabled us all to connect within seconds, all through the power of mobile and the internet. The rise of social applications means we are communicating as a collective with the ability to influence on a mass scale. Over the next decade or two we will see an even faster advancement in technology, and greater connectivity, but this inadvertently means an even higher rate of competition.

Those businesses with common aims should stick together; they must collaborate and share resources. Brand sharing and benefiting from each other's proposition will start to take more and more prominence. For those businesses that want to not only survive but thrive in the 21st century market, Partnership Marketing is the answer.

What will you get out of this book?

With so few text books, reading materials and online content available, this leaves us with an essential need for a detailed guide. This book aims to provide a complete explanation of Partnership Marketing, outlining all the specifics and describing how you can undertake it in your own business.

This book is a step-by-step guide of how to run Partnership Marketing campaigns. The sequence of chapters explains what Partnership Marketing is and the distinct types, before taking you through how to formulate partnerships, managing those relationships, deciding objectives and running joint campaigns. The aim is to provide you with more than just theory, but give you the necessary skills to create partnership campaigns. The techniques described have been tried and tested via years of experience in the field.

Importantly I aim to explain how to run your partnerships in both offline and online capacities. I have placed a prominence on digital practices as to highlight its importance in today's marketing, without ignoring the offline benefits.

Finally, I hope it provides you with everything you are looking for on the topic, whether you are interested in learning about an emerging type of marketing, or looking to grow your own Partnership Marketing channel. I hope it increases your knowledge on the topic, helps advance your careers and delivers success in your marketing practices, while bringing Partnership Marketing into the mainstream where it rightly belongs.

2. WHAT IS PARTNERSHIP MARKETING?

Partnership Marketing is often referred to as Joint Marketing, Co-Marketing or Merchant Marketing, although Partnership is now the more universally accepted term.

Definition

Partnership Marketing has been defined multiple times and in many different guises, but in its simplest form can be described as:

Where two or more brands collaborate via strategic marketing campaigns to promote their products or services to their respective audiences to achieve their marketing objectives.

The 10 Types

These are the most common forms of Partnership Marketing practiced today. While one model might be suitable for one company it may not necessary fit into the scope for another. Brands may decide to use one or to use many, or combine several to form a hybrid. The 10 types are not fixed, they are fluid and interchangeable depending on the partnership in question.

1. **Affiliation** - a performance marketing activity that allows your products or services to be advertised across affiliated websites. Popular brands such as [1]Amazon run affiliate programmes that encourage publisher sites to promote their goods in return for a share of the sale value. Alternatively, brands can join affiliate networks who then distribute the services to potentially thousands of publishers.

2. **Content** - where both partners agree to create and share new and engaging content to attract the attention of the target audience. This is a popular Partnership Marketing technique when it comes to search engine optimisation (SEO) and enhancing a brand via viral campaigns.

3. **Distribution** - where one partner agrees to distribute another's products or services. The primary brand often agrees to provide its distribution channels for the secondary, utilising its supplier and sales streams.

4. **Charitable** - the act of partnering with a charitable organisation. When it comes to Partnership Marketing this can be utilised to enhance brand reputation. [2]FC Barcelona featuring UNICEF on their football jerseys was a good example of this.

5. **Joint Products** - when two brands agree to create a new product or alter an existing one to provide a unique offering for the consumer. The joint product can be a unification of both brands or the alteration of the primary to feature the secondary.

6. **Licensing** - when a popular brand sells their name for use on merchandise or goods. The image or brand is utilised to enhance the product offering.

7. **Loyalty** - the act of offering your customers additional value for increased use of their goods or services. It is a highly effective type of Partnership Marketing and one of the more common employed by brands today.

8. **Product Placement** - where a brand places their product or service within media such as television, film or music videos. The placement is made where the brand is subtly shown in the scene or storyline.

9. **Shared-Stores** - where a brand agrees to share a portion of their store with another to improve customer experience and product reach. This is popular with coffee shops, such as Starbucks, as well as petrol stations and cinemas.

10. **Sponsorship** - one of the most popular forms of Partnership Marketing aligning your brand with events or organisations

such as the Olympic Games, Football Leagues or Music Festivals.

Terminology

Alongside the 10 types of Partnership Marketing it's important to understand the terminology that goes with them. Although similar, there are slight difference between each term. Here are the definitions for each:

- **In Partnership With** - the most popular phrase used to describe a partnership with another brand. It informs consumers that there is a collaboration occurring and that the partnership will benefit both brands as well as ultimately the consumer.

- **Supported By** - commonly found within charitable partnerships. Being supported by a partner refers to one brand assisting the other in the campaign. It portrays an element of trust towards a consumer, showing the cause is backed by a reputable brand.

- **Certified By** - provides authenticity to the partnership. By stating that a brand certifies another delivers reassurance to the consumer that the offering is backed by the supporting brand.

- **Incorporating** - if a major brand is incorporating with another it is referencing the fact that they are providing their services as an add-on or an extra.

- **Powered By** - refers to the presence of a partner brand supplying their services to benefit another product. An example of this is the [3]Nexus phone which is 'Powered by' Google. Such a partnership ultimately benefits the consumer with a far superior product utilising both technologies.

- **In Association With** - most commonly used when both brands have an equal role to play in the partnership. The term association means that both brands have agreed on a mutual offering.

<u>Example</u>

Virgin Media offers Netflix to Consumers

[4]Virgin Media is a provider of broadband, TV and mobile phone.[5]Netflix is one of the world's largest on-demand Internet streaming media services, available in the US, Europe, and Asia.

[6]Their partnership formulated in 2013 where Virgin Media integrated the Netflix option within the network. This meant that Virgin Media viewers could easily browse Netflix's acclaimed line-up across Virgin TV's entire choice of entertainment.

It is a fine use of Partnership Marketing with Virgin's subsequent marketing campaigns displaying both brands side by side to highlight the exclusive offering.

Difference between Business and Marketing Partnerships

Many professionals unfamiliar with Partnership Marketing still believe it is the same as a business merger or company acquisition, whereas this simply isn't the case. The word 'Partnership' is often incorrectly mentioned when referencing a company takeover. Descriptions such as 'the two companies will now merge and collaborate towards a common goal' is often misconstrued as a partnership.

Partnership Marketing is not about the merging or joining of companies under one venture, there should always be independence between both parties. When mentioned throughout this book the focus is on the marketing of both brands collaborating towards mutual goals. It is leveraging each other's customer base, attracting new customers or retaining existing through added value. A 'strategic alliance' or 'merger' on the other hand is concentrated around two companies becoming one under a single umbrella. There is therefore a significant difference between the two.

As mentioned in the opening chapter, companies do often decide to 'partner' in a strategic sense and not necessarily merge with or acquire one another. This is also not the same as Partnership Marketing though sometimes these strategic business partnerships can result in it. The purpose here is to recognise what is a marketing partnership.

Example

Healthy Living with the Pruhealth and Virgin Active Partnership

[7]Pruhealth operating under their sub-brand VitalityHealth is one of the UK's leading Health Insurance providers. Their motto is to reward members for living well. An active lifestyle will bring you a collection of exclusive rewards via recognisable brands they have partnered with such as Cineworld, Evans Cycles and Lloyds Pharmacy.

[8]Virgin Active is considered one of the largest global health clubs operating in South Africa, Spain, Singapore and the UK. Founded by Sir Richard Branson it is as one of the corner-stones of the global Virgin brand. Their slogan is to 'live happily ever active', not too dissimilar to the Pruhealth living well motto.

[9]Pruhealth offers their customers 50% off Virgin Active monthly memberships. This offering can only be found exclusively through the VitalityHealth programme. It shows how both brands can partner solely for marketing purposes rather than merging or acquiring one another. [10]

What are the benefits of Partnership Marketing?

There is an ever-increasing necessity for Partnership Marketing in today's business world. As our global network continues to connect, and so companies ever more reachable, partnering will become increasingly important.

Before we illustrate the benefits of Partnership Marketing, let's take a step back and consider what the benefits of marketing are. Marketing is the actions taken to aid the selling of a product or service. These actions include what we know as the 4P's of Marketing - The Marketing Mix, which we come onto in more detail in the next section. These 4P's; Placement, Pricing, Product and Promotion defines a company's marketing. Getting these right leads to increasing sales, improved brand recognition and overall company growth.

The Main Benefits

As an emerging marketing technique, Partnership Marketing has its own set of specific benefits. These will differ from firm to firm but collectively follow similar themes. In essence, it is of huge advantage to every business that undertakes it. Partnership Marketing:

- Enables brands to reach partner brand target audiences
- Leverages another brand's assets
- Improves brand image by collaborating with a reputable partner
- Generates new revenue streams
- Increases customer retention due to partner association
- Sparks innovation via new product synergies
- Grows the network of stakeholders and industry contacts
- Provides added value to consumers through exclusivity
- Lowers barriers to entry and grows market share
- Lowers cost per acquisition via cost-effective sharing of resources
- Enhances distribution channels and product offerings
- Improves employee satisfaction via charitable association

Brands, more than ever, are looking for new avenues for commercial value and to diversify distribution channels to increase growth and acquire new customers. By collaborating with like-minded brands, whose audience will engage and resonate with the offer, could only lead to success and all round mutual gain.

Comparing with other Marketing Channels

To start with, let's say that comparing marketing channels or techniques is extremely subjective. We cannot say if Email Marketing or Social Media will be more effective without knowing the marketing strategy and objectives of the campaign you're working on. This also applies to Partnership Marketing, how much value it adds entirely depends on the task in question.

The Six Main Marketing Objectives

Before exploring this further, we should ask ourselves what is it we want to achieve from our marketing? The majority of marketing strategies, and subsequent campaigns, aim towards one or more of the following objectives:

1. New Customer Acquisition
2. Increase Customer Spend/Basket Size
3. Increase Customer Spend Frequency
4. Reactivation of Dormant Customers
5. Brand Awareness and Exposure
6. Generating Revenue through Advertising Commission

Common Marketing Channels

In order to achieve your chosen objectives, marketing departments tend to focus their resources upon the following channels. From here we can begin to understand where Partnership Marketing adds value:

- **Email Marketing** - one of the most efficient methods for businesses to communicate with their customers. It is a vital component of every marketing strategy.

- **Digital Marketing** - incorporates all digital practises such as SEO, PPC, Display and Retargeting. This is arguably the single most important channel at a marketing department's disposal right now. The return on investment is both visible and easily trackable.

- **Social Media** - often incorporated as part of Digital Marketing, it involves the utilisation of networks such as Facebook and Twitter to engage with customers and prospect new acquisitions.

- **PR** - involves the management of your external reputation and influencing this via relevant publications. Often dramatised with the term 'PR Stunts' used by some brands for brand elevation.

- **Events** - provides 'on the ground' interaction, thought-leadership and public awareness. A channel that can be vital for personal engagement with your customer base and building relationships.

- **Mobile Marketing** - the concept of promoting your services via mobile optimised and responsive devices, as well as Application (apps) creation and advertising.

These channels are just some but not all the ones used by marketers to achieve their strategy. What is noticeable is that rarely do they stand on their own. Marketers often use a combination of these marketing channels to achieve their objectives.

This brings us onto Partnership Marketing, which I feel should not be classed alongside these channels. Partnerships are more of a technique and can be used as part of any of the above, or encompass them all. Partnership Marketing shouldn't replace Email or PR, instead when it comes to campaign planning and execution, it should be considered so to get the best out of these channels.

Where Partnership Marketing fits into your Business

Nokia, Apple, Nike, O2, Barclays, PayPal, American Express and John Lewis are just some of the big-name brands partaking in Partnership Marketing today. As its popularity grows the necessity for it to have a distinct place in companies is becoming more apparent.

Team Responsibilities

Such companies are creating Partnership Marketing teams to undertake several core responsibilities, such as handling partner relationships and execute marketing initiatives. This also includes the recruitment of relevant partners, deciding which will resonate with the target audience, allocating assets and developing innovative campaigns.

Team Personnel

A Partnership Marketing team can vary in size depending on the organisation, often sitting as its own sub-team within a marketing department. Some firms tend to place it as a go-between amid Account Management and Affiliate Marketing.

Most teams are run by a Head of Partnership Marketing, with succeeding Managers and Executives depending on the business size and the number of people involved. The Head is responsible for focusing on high-level strategic planning, while the other roles focus on daily account management of partners and campaign execution. A successful team is one that manages existing partners, prospects new ones, executes requests and organises strategic campaigns efficiently to achieve their set objectives.

Uniquely Placed

Partnership Marketing is a business function which is uniquely placed within the organisation. The unit handles partner relationships alongside marketing of the products which means there is a lot of cross-departmental responsibilities. Anyone working in Partnership

Marketing must therefore have the skillset to manage relationships both internally and externally. It must be an adaptable team, one that can manage a huge range of requests, can seek out opportunities and be open to new ideas and innovations.

Responsibilities and Attributes of a successful Partnership Marketing Manager

Whether you are already a member of a Partnership Marketing team, or looking to set up one at your own company, there are a number of specific responsibilities and attributes required to manage it successfully.

Key Responsibilities

- **Account Management** - a successful Partnership Marketing Manager needs to be able to manage relationships. Dealing with so many different partners, brands and people daily is a multi-tasking skill that is pivotal to the role.

- **Drive Sales** - every Partnership marketer must also possess excellent sales skills. Selling the value proposition and brand to potential partners is a key responsibility.

- **Achieve Objectives** - as outlined there are six main marketing objectives and Partnership Marketing can target any of them. They must strive towards their set objectives during campaign creation and execution.

- **Understanding Marketing Techniques** - needs to have an excellent grasp of all marketing techniques and channels, as Partnership Marketing can reach out across every type.

- **Create and Execute Campaigns** - partnership campaigns rely on a creative thinker, one who can innovatively produce a campaign encompassing both parties, and execute it efficiently.

- **Track and Analyse Campaigns** - needs to ensure sufficient tracking is in place and analyse campaigns effectively, comparing results to forecasts. Accuracy and precision in this area will lead to successful campaigns.

- **Briefing Agencies** - Partnership Marketing managers work alongside either an in-house design team or specialist agencies when it comes to creating campaign components. Briefing exact specifications is an important aspect of the role.

- **Recruit New Partners** - there is also the need to acquire new relationships. This means to seek and prospect new partner brands.

- **Industry Awareness** - every Partnership manager needs to have their eyes and ears on the industry, paying attention to those collaborating, as well as those competing.

- **Retain Reputation** - as this role means working with a huge array of external contacts, the reputation of a business can lay in your hands. A Partnership Marketing manager can be the external face of a brand, so must uphold the company's reputation.

- **Team Management** - not only do they need to manage the personnel within the Partnerships team, but this role must also manage the partners themselves.

Essential Attributes

As the role covers so many areas, the Partnership Marketing manager should possess many of these key attributes:

- **Multitasking** - multiple requests, multiple partners and multiple departments to work with means it is vital to be able multi-task. Not only do you need to manage and organise your own time, but also organise each partner and their respective campaign.

- **Marketing Knowledge** - as we referenced above a Partnership Marketer will be utilising most marketing channels, therefore excellent knowledge of each is fundamental.

- **Analytical skills** - campaigns must be forecasted and analysed in order to provide accurate results to senior stakeholders.

- **Communication Skills** - a strong Partnership Marketer is one that possesses fluid communication skills, as the role requires regular interaction across multiple stakeholders. It is important to be able to build a rapport with external clients in order to create strong and lasting relationships.

- **Unclouded Judgement** - the ability to siphon out the good from the bad using logical thinking so the right partner can be chosen, correct campaigns be decided upon and the right approach always be taken.

- **Targets Driven** - needs to be focused on achieving the forecasted results with every step of the campaign.

- **Negotiation Skills** - strong negotiation skills are important to achieve the best possible outcome for your company. It is important to be able to persuade partners into securing the best prices and asset positions, while keeping a good relationship.

- **Presentation Skills** - presenting to partners involves strong communication skills and the ability to sell. It may also include creating a PowerPoint presentation with an engaging pitch.

- **Creativity** - Partnership Marketing requires 'out-of-the-box' thinking. This means creating imaginative campaigns to draw in new customers.

Job Description Example

To give a better idea of what the role entails, and what most businesses look for in an individual, below is a typical example of a Partnership Marketing Manager's job description:

Overview:

- *The Partnership Marketing Manager is a key commercial role responsible for developing new marketing channels through partnerships and managing a range of marketing relationships with partner brands, and supporting the overall integrated sales and marketing plan.*

- *This person is key to delivering on all aspects of the growth ambitions of the Partnerships channel and is a critical role within the commercial marketing and acquisition team.*

Responsibilities:

- *To drive new customer acquisition via partnership marketing campaigns with our partner brands and affiliates.*
- *Creation and running of all campaigns, including the production of campaign and design briefs, planning, execution and analysis of campaign results.*
- *Creation and execution of all partner communications to actively engage with our customer base, and promote our respective partners.*
- *Responsible for managing and growing all promotional assets and advertising collateral.*
- *Involves the management of all partnership marketing relationships, negotiation of improved affiliation agreements and management of all promotional collateral.*
- *Develops a monthly dashboard of statistics, recording and summarising all monthly statistics and performance against annual revenue forecasts.*
- *Updating key stakeholders on results, presenting to the board on the success or failures of such partnerships.*
- *Responsible for recruiting new partner. Involves continuous communications with new respective leads, negotiating new agreements and improving their accounts.*
- *Responsible for ongoing engagement with the business unit Heads of Marketing, as well as Account Management teams in order to understand their respective targets, plans and how the partnership marketing strategy will assist their forecasted results.*
- *Manages external agency resources (email service provider, design/creative, publications etc.) to ensure campaigns are executed on time, on budget and to high quality.*
- *Management of the partnership marketing team including two executives.*

Preferred Attributes:

- *Extensive partnership marketing management experience, gained from significant tenures at well-respected brands.*
- *Test and Learn mind-set, with experience of A-B testing across multiple channels*
- *Strong campaign, project and budget management skills.*
- *Excellent briefing and agency/supplier management skills.*
- *Both Digital Marketing and Offline Marketing experience highly desirable.*
- *Commercially astute and proven focus on the achievement of positive ROI.*
- *Tenacious, overcomes barriers to effective working methods with a continuous improvement.*

- *Excellent communication and presentation skills, with a proven ability to engage and influence at senior management/board level.*
- *Experience and strong understanding of the associated industry*
- *Marketing degree or similar.*

3. TYPES OF PARTNERSHIP MARKETING

Affiliation

Of the 10 types of Partnership Marketing, arguably Affiliate Marketing is the more prominent. It is now an extremely prevalent and prosperous online tactic which has spawned an entire industry of agencies, networks and programmes in a relatively short space of time.

Definition

Affiliate Marketing is a performance marketing technique where websites, otherwise known as publishers, will promote your product or service in return for a monetary reward.

Types

Affiliate Marketing can be achieved by using any of the methods described below. Both utilise a primary partner (often referred to as an advertiser - the business supplying the advertisement of their brand) and a secondary partner (often referred to as the affiliate or the publisher - those that are willing to advertise a primary brand by publishing it on their website) working in collaboration. In doing so, the advertiser benefits from promotion of their products resulting in sales, whilst the publisher benefits from commissions.

1. **In-House** - when an advertiser is looking for a solution that provides them with the ability to upload all creative banners, select relevant tracking links and display all results in one centralised location, they use an affiliate program. An In-House program is often favoured in certain industries, as it offers an easy and ready to use solution. Providers such as [11]CAKE and [12]Income Access offer a plug-in option, while companies such as Amazon have built their own.

2. **Networks** - a third party where both advertiser and publisher register and utilise its services all through the Network's portal. A major benefit to brands over an In-House solution is that it

provides far greater reach for publishers to find relevant brands to promote, while the advertiser is immediately exposed to thousands of publisher sites rather than having to promote their own In-house programme. A simple way of visualising this is as a market place for affiliates. Examples include [13]Linkshare, [14]Commission Junction, and [15]Affiliate Window.

3. **Agencies** - a third option for businesses are to work directly with an agency which manages the portfolio of affiliates, as well as the admin behind it such as banners and tracking links. Ultimately, they should support your requirements and are seen as an attractive option to those without the expertise or time.

Forms

Affiliates can promote an advertiser using numerous techniques. Depending on the type of website, unique selling point (USP) and target audience, they will promote those with the highest conversion and those offering the greatest commission rates:

- **Banner Advertisement** - are one of the more common forms of exposure for a partner brand on a publisher site. Header (728x90) or Skyscraper (160x600) banners are most popular.

- **Text Link** - a native hyperlink found within an article. It is subtler than a banner ad.

- **Dedicated Article** - a strong partnership between brands can lead to more unique forms of exposure. A dedicated article can engage a target audience and provide a more detailed product description than that of a text link or banner ad.

- **Dedicated Page/Tab** - expanding the concept a publisher can also create a dedicated page or section of their site specifically for the advertiser.

- **Promotional Page** - exposure of advertisers through specific areas of the publisher's site devoted to promotional offers. Here banner ads can be kept separate from the core content.

- **Newsletters** - for those affiliates that require accounts to be created or email addresses to be captured, newsletters are a strategic way for them to directly market affiliate offers. [16]Groupon and [17]Quidco for example are excellent at targeting their database with the latest partner deals.

- **Comparison Table** - for aggregator sites such as [18]Moneysupermarket.com and [19]Confused.com the comparison table is a huge USP. It allows them to rank advertisers by pricing, features and benefits, as well those offering highest commission returns.

<u>Understanding</u>

Affiliate Marketing is widely considered to be one of the purest forms of Partnership Marketing. It is also referred to as Performance Marketing because it can be so accurately measured and the return on investment (ROI) precisely calculated. Affiliation is quantifiable and unlike other marketing methods can always be proven.

Affiliation refers to the practice of partner websites promoting your brand in return for commissions. An affiliate will be paid depending on the agreement that has been made with the advertiser. It is not always a complete sale, there are many models that pay based on the number of impressions, clicks or leads. The types of commission structures are CPM (cost per thousand impression), CPC (cost per click), CPA (cost per acquisition), Revenue Share (percentage of the revenue a sale generates) or a Fixed Fee. There are also amalgamations of these referred to as Hybrids.

An affiliate can range from a well-known newspaper brand, such as [20]The Daily Mail, to a small one-man-band website reviewing headphones. Both follow the same principle as they contain content, attract traffic and publish ads. There are many affiliate variants out there; voucher sites such as Groupon, cashback sites such as [21]TopCashback, or aggregator sites such as MoneySupermarket.com or [22]Gocompare.

Bringing this back to Partnership Marketing, when primary brands are looking for specific partners to promote their services, affiliation is a very attractive option. It creates an alliance in a direct way towards a mutual target audience. [23]LG for example, the popular TV manufacture, will work closely with renowned TV review sites to drive sales. The review site will demonstrate the quality of the brand offering and effectively promote LG's products to their database.

Example

Here is an example that gives a clear indication of how Affiliate Partnerships executed effectively benefits both parties:

- **Money.co.uk & IG** - [24]Money.co.uk is one of the most popular money comparison websites in the world. It provides a useful service to its users and in turn generates revenues from promoting partners as an affiliate. [25]IG is one of the largest investment firms out there. Here they have worked directly with IG to place them at the top of their Investment ISA table. They encourage users to click-through to IG, in return receiving commission per new customer. IG benefits from the sale made via Money.co.uk's affiliation. [26]

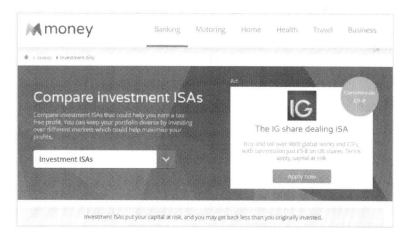

Content

The web is made up of content, and search engines, namely [27]Google, who try to make sense of it. Search Engine Optimisation (SEO), the ranking of websites, is based on the relevance of the content your site comprises of, making it imperative to its visibility and therefore success.

All sites are aiming to improve their content to drive traffic via these engines, always looking to add fresh, innovative and hopefully viral additions. New content is shared, linked, liked and tweeted to potential new consumers every second of every day all over the world.

One of the most innovative ways to create and distribute this is via a partner brand, making Content Partnerships one of the fastest growing strands of Partnership Marketing.

Definition

Content Marketing is the creation of relevant content that will be highly engaging to customers. Content Partnerships are the development of such content in collaboration with a partner brand that is then shared or promoted to respective target audiences.

Types

There are two main ways a brand can partake in Content Partnerships:

1. **Co-Creation** - both brands collaborate to create the content. This could be industry trends, market research, product releases or thought-leadership papers. By writing the content together, and referencing one another's products, it will align both brands for mutual recognition.

2. **Link Sharing** - the primary brand creates the content but works in partnership with a secondary to promote it. Link sharing means linking to the partner's content from their own

site. This provides exposure, aligns both brands together and advances SEO.

Forms

Content Partnerships can take various formats, below are some of the most common:

- **White Papers** - presenting the latest industry research, advice, knowledge and trends using thought-leadership.

- **Articles** - featuring the latest joint products, opinions or promotions. These can take the form of reviews, how-to guides, case-studies, editorials or advertorials.

- **Infographics** - a visual representation of information or data. This is effective for the use of joint brand imagery.

- **Videos & Podcasts** - the joint creation of a video or spoken media. Utilising the likes of [28]YouTube to engage with the target audience.

Understanding

Search Engine Optimisation is now such an important aspect of digital marketing that specialist agencies have arisen. The success in search rankings could make or break a business, making it the 21st centuries most talked about marketing topic.

The evolution of websites has now reached the point where each page should ultimately evoke an action encouraging customers down the conversion funnel. The greater the numbers to a site, the better the chance of conversions and therefore revenues. This is the reason millions are spent climbing the ladder of Google's rankings.

Organic traffic via SEO is governed by a complex, well-guarded algorithm made up of a huge number of variables, such as keywords, inbound links and subject relevance. This means that your 'content is king'; how it is constructed, who likes it and how it is shared has direct influence on traffic, conversions and ultimately sales.

SEO is not the only means to achieving traffic, social media has a huge part to play too. Facebook and Twitter can guide vast quantities of traffic to your site depending on what you have to say and how engaging your content is.

To ensure traffic remains high from both SEO and social, the information that consumers receive must be fresh, relevant and engaging. It also must answer their questions, fulfil their needs and attract their attention. This is where Content Partnership Marketing comes in.

Providing fresh material in conjunction with a partner can make it far more interesting, likeable and engaging. This will attract a much larger network that will interact and share it. The utilisation of one another's digital channels and expertise also means a lower cost per acquisition per content piece produced.

Example

Brands are quickly catching onto the idea of Content Partnership Marketing, below an example from two well-known brands:

- **Lonely Planet and British Airways** - [29]British Airways teamed up with Lonely Planet to inspire consumers with a series of tempting travel adventures. The series, 'Ultimate Experiences', highlighted easy-to-reach short haul destinations. The partnership ran for 12 weeks and featured destinations ranging from Paris to Marrakesh. The partnership provided bite sized pieces of content that, via research undertaken by both companies, showed what the on-the-move consumer preferred and typically engaged with. It shows how two well-known brands in the travel industry can come together to create new joint content that engages the consumer. [30]

Lonely Planet Ultimate Experiences

British Airways has teamed up with Lonely Planet to inspire passengers on the London Underground with a series of tempting travel adventures.

The series, Ultimate Experiences, will run every Monday, all day, on 60 x XTP screens across zones 1 & 2 and will recommend a different easy-to-reach short haul destination each week. The activity will run for a 12 week period and feature destinations ranging from Salzburg to Marrakesh.

Research shows that Tube users are hungry for short form content on the go, making the XTP screens the perfect platform to reach BA's younger, experience-loving target audience.

Distribution

Distribution Partnership Marketing is one of the most effective ways for a brand to reach their target audience. It is deemed highly effective because it physically puts a partner brand in the hands of new customers.

Definition

Where one partner agrees to cross-market or package another partner's product or services into their own distribution channels to target the agreed customer base.

Type

There is one main type of Distribution Partnership Marketing, found both offline and offline, and that is insertion. Used in various forms as described below it essentially describes the insertion of a partner brand within your distribution channels. If you primarily sell your products via post for example, then including a packaged bundle of a partner's product is a great way to market theirs, or vice versa.

Forms

There are many distinct ways in which to distribute a partner brand to provide the most effective customer targeting:

- In-Store Leaflets
- In-Store Coupons
- Magazine Coupons
- In-Store Live Demonstrations
- In-Store TV Demonstrations
- Email Vouchers
- Mobile Coupons
- QR Codes

Understanding

Distribution has been practiced for decades. Before the digital age, offering your product via the distribution channels of another company was seen as a popular method of spreading your product to new markets. Although newer types of Partnership Marketing have emerged, Distribution is still popular as it physically and visually places the partner brands alongside each other and in the hands of the target audience.

Example

The nature of these partnerships means that cases are predominantly offline. Below is one such example of a collaboration:

- **Domino's Pizza & Virgin Wines** - [31]In 2009 popular pizza delivery chain Domino's partnered with the Virgin Wines club as part of its efforts to appeal to a wider range of customers and offer an upmarket dining experience. Customers could get a whole range of boutique wine discounts or Virgin Wines subscriptions with certain Domino's pizza orders. The partnership helped distribute the Virgin Wines offering via the Domino's delivery service. Both firms promoted the offering the tie up across their online platforms, email marketing, direct mail and the Virgin Wines blog.

Charitable

With Charitable Marketing Partnerships, a brand associates itself with a charity for the purposes of promotion and recognition. The act of working with a charity has been a traditional aspect of corporate responsibility, aiming to give back to the community.

It is important to note that this is not the same as a Corporate Partnership. [32]Corporate Partnerships are where organisations provide funds, skills and resources to a charity, while we are referring to the marketing opportunities within such a collaboration.

Definition

A primary brand sponsors or markets itself with a charitable organisation or cause. In turn, they seek exposure and promotion via agreed marketing channels.

Benefits

Two main reasons why a primary brand would have a Charitable Marketing Partnership:

1. **Cultural Influence** - a brand can primarily work as a moral and responsible contributor, seeking to collaborate due to the attitudes of senior stakeholders and influence on internal company culture.

2. **Brand Leverage** - some firms prefer to associate themselves to a charity due to the benefits it brings to their consumer and public reputation.

Forms

Charitable Partnerships can take a variety of forms, these represent various ways that a brand and charity can run campaigns together:

- Exhibitions
- Public Events
- Award Shows

- Sponsorship
- Raffle Contributions
- News Stories
- Sporting Events

Understanding

As today's customer is more industry aware and savvy with their purchasing decisions than ever before, with abundant comparison and review sites at their fingertips, a brand that upholds a strong public reputation is becoming increasingly important to stand out from the competition. Associating your brand to a charitable cause is therefore fast becoming the main method to securing a reputable status.

[33]Innocent Smoothies for example, one of the most reputable drinks companies in the UK, stress the importance of fair-trade production. They also associate themselves with a number of charities via their Innocent Foundation. Firms such as this that leverage Charitable Marketing Partnerships could see their public reputation and brand image enhanced.

Example

The finest partnerships propel a brand's image and reputation, as shown in the below example:

- **Sainsbury's and Red Nose Day** - [34]Comic Relief is a British charity that appeals through their Red Nose Day telethons to raise money for global famines. [35]Sainsbury's, a major partner since 1999, raising over £95M, help to promote the event by selling the Red Noses, as well as a host of other merchandise. From a marketing perspective they also benefit from exposure across the Red Nose Day event and gain an enhanced brand reputation. [36]

Joint Products

Joint Product Partnerships are generally considered the most innovative of all collaboration types. They emerge between two organisations who agree to create a new product or combine their existing ones. Both aim to complement one another to add value for the consumer.

Definition

When two companies agree to create a new or alter an existing product in order to provide additional value to the customer. Often the product is an amalgamation of both products.

Types

For brands partaking in Joint Product Partnerships there are many factors to consider. Bearing in mind the huge impact on internal product departments, they are presented with four main choices:

1. **Powered By** - a partner brand supplying their services or software to benefit a new or existing product. Mobile phones powered by a technology provider such as Google or Microsoft is a good example.

2. **White Label** - many successful technologies also offer white label solutions. This means selling off their services to a partner brand. The partner brand then utilises the technology under its own name.

3. **Product Merger** - a merger is where both brands have decided to amalgamate their products together. This too comes in various formats, from full to partial mergers depending on the product line.

4. **Integration** - in similar fashion to 'powered by', a partner may wish to integrate another brand into their own. Rather than utilising its technology, instead utilising an API integration to offer an additional service to the existing one.

Forms

These alliances can be very interesting for an organisation's product portfolio, as it results in a fresh line of innovative product solutions. With the breakthrough of digital technologies over the past two decades we are now seeing a far greater increase in such partnerships. There are four specific forms that have emerged:

- **New Product Launch** - two firms may decide to launch a brand-new product, one that amalgamates both under an exciting new concept. Both companies leverage each other's brand image, reputation, resources, and market reach.

- **Brand Leveraging** - rather than a full product merger often just the branding is joined. With such product partnerships it is about utilising the partners design and packaging.

- **New Markets** - by merging products together a popular firm in the US seeking new customers from Europe might collaborate with a successful European brand to enter this new market.

- **Sharing Costs** - occasionally a Product Partnership will purely be a cost-saving exercise. This is achieved with the sharing of resources and expertise, this in turn reduces cost of production and marketing.

Understanding

The main consideration with this partnership is that it is both a product and marketing initiative, involving the buy-in from both departments. Any alterations to a product would also need to be briefed to the sales departments. There are also costs and resources to be considered when producing something completely new.

An effective go-to-market strategy will require a distinct value proposition. The unique selling point of the joint product must be communicated to highlight these new product features and their benefits. Branding is also important, getting this right will ensure that the primary brand's look and feel is displayed, not only through the packaging but also via all advertising.

However, this type of Partnership Marketing doesn't come without its complications. If producing something completely new misses the mark, and the value proposition fails to resonate with the target audience, it would certainly be deemed a very expensive failure.

Examples

As technology continues to improve, the opportunities for successful product collaborations will continue to grow. Here are two examples of successful Joint Product Partnerships:

- **LG & Prada -** [37]Prada is one of the most recognised fashion labels in the world. Their brand resonates class and prestige. LG Electronics are also an upmarket brand, but in the technology, electronics and mobile phone industry. In 2006 LG teamed up with Prada to tap into the growing high-end mobile phone market with their "Prada phone by LG". This is an example of two successful companies coming together to produce a new unique offering for their customers.

- **Nike & Apple -** [38]In 2006 Apple and Nike demonstrated one of the finest examples of Joint Product Partnerships. 'The Nike

& iPod Sports Kit' was stored in your shoe and measured the distance of your runs, sending the information directly to your iPod. Since then further adaptions were produced including the Nike Running App which leverages this devise further. [39]

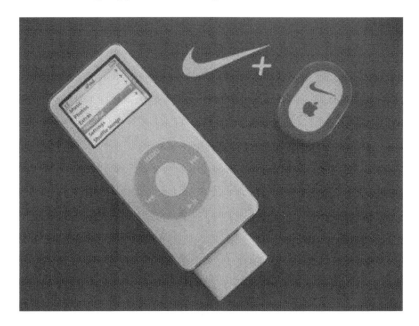

Licensing

Licensing is a huge industry, though one which is rarely talked about. It is the act of a brand selling the use of their name and imagery to another brand.

Definition

Licensing is a business arrangement in which one company gives another company permission to manufacture its product using its brand image for an agreed payment or partnership.

Types

There are two ways that a brand will choose to collaborate with another when it comes to Licensing Partnership Marketing:

1. **Sold** - companies that decide to sell their brands to other companies for a given price. This provides the purchaser access to the different forms (described below) to improve their product or service offering.

2. **Collaborative** - some brands decide to get more involved in the licensing partnership and actively collaborate with the partner with how their brand should be used. This has close associations with Joint Product Partnerships where both companies work together on an exclusive unique offering.

Forms

There are many ways a company who licenses another's brand can utilise it. After purchasing the right to use their brand they can work on the following:

- **Logo** - the logo of another brand can be used within a company's own product line to enhance it.

- **Brand Image** - the brand image itself can comprise not only the logo but the colours, font and tone of voice.

- **Reputation** - with the purchase of any brand comes with it its reputation; utilising this to a company's advantage in their new product offering.

- **Culture** - with a brands reputation also comes its company culture. A company can utilise the ethics and company values this also brings.

- **Design** - the shapes, styles and characters that come with a brand can also be utilised within the firm's products or services.

Understanding

The creation of a brand, one with a stand out reputation, is extremely time consuming and costly, so for many organisations the quickest and simplest way is to purchase someone else's. This is what licensing offers a company; tying in a global brand to the product hugely enhances it.

A product can go from mediocre to a sales success very swiftly if the right brand is licensed effectively. Simply using another brands name for the product and attaching the logo to it, even if the product hasn't changed at all from previous editions, can lead to a huge surge in sales.

Example

Licensing agreements usually involve popular brands we know and love. It can be a big financial advantage to organisations who sell off their branding. Below is an example of one such recognisable agreement:

- **Angry Birds and Star Wars** - [40]Angry Birds is one of the world's most prosperous gaming applications and employs a successful strategy of releasing new versions of its game to keep the brand fresh and maintain its popularity. An example of this was its Star Wars Licensing Partnership, one of the most iconic movie brand of all time, in an agreement which meant the Star Wars brand could be adapted for the Angry Birds game.

Loyalty

Loyalty is vital for the livelihood of all major brands and one of the key influential factors on customer retention rates. It is the personal connection a consumer has towards a brand and the rates in which they continue to purchase.

Definition

A retention marketing technique that offers consumers a reward in return for increased usage. A loyalty partnership offers consumers partner rewards to encourage longevity and purchase frequency.

Types

Loyalty Partnership Marketing comes in 3 specific types. All of which relate to how consumers are loyal to a brand:

1. **Frequency** - loyalty can be rewarded based on frequency of customer use; the more a product is bought, or a service used, the more rewards a consumer receives. A reward can be a partner brand discount. Smart brands take this a step further by personalising; providing an offer in conjunction with a partner brand which is tailored to the consumer based on their spending patterns or profile.

2. **Volume** - the alternative is to reward based on amount purchased; where the higher the number bought the larger the reward. Savvy brands provide varying degrees of reward to those that purchase larger amounts, often fully personalising the offer.

3. **Advocate** - the third type is often described as advocacy; where a consumer is so loyal to a brand they will support it and promote it, and in return a brand will offer extended rewards. It is a type of loyalty that focuses purely on rewarding those who shout about a brand and even have the power to influence others (explained more in the Influencers section).

Forms

Here we have outlined some of the more popular ways a brand can encourage consumer loyalty. The different forms can be adjusted depending on consumer base segments:

- Loyalty Club/Scheme
- Loyalty Cards/Vouchers
- One off Rewards
- Free Money, Gifts, Raffles
- Seasonal Promotions
- Product Extensions

These all offer the possibility for partner brand involvement, mainly by including their discounts or exclusive products within the loyalty program.

Understanding

As a technique it allows two brands to successfully align their offering to improve customer retention rates. This is a type of Partnership Marketing that has been tried and tested by a number of high profile brand names such as Tesco and PayPal.

A loyal collaboration can enhance the image of a brand, acquire a vast number of new customers, and can increase spend frequency and volume growth.

Example

Loyalty Partnership Marketing can be found in abundance, both online and offline. Below is one such big name example:

- **British Airways and American Express** - [41]American Express encourage their holders to spend more in return for points which can then be converted into air miles. Here they have teamed up with one of the biggest names in the aviation industry, British Airways, to provide such an offering. [42]

Product Placement

We frequently see brands appear within our TV programmes and films, this is commonly referred to as Product Placement. It is a long-standing medium of Partnership Marketing as brands aim to leverage the advertising potential of high profile media.

Definition

The subtle placement of a brand within a media channel. It is deemed a cross-over of sponsorship and advertising that works well in partnership with high grossing TV and film productions.

Types

There are three types of Product Placement Partnership Marketing. These reflect the main ways in which products are placed within the media, a decision made through the coalition of brand and media channel:

1. **Subtle Placement** - where the inclusion of the brand logo, such as the product placed in the background, is found within TV and film scenes.

2. **Direct Advertising** - aside from Subtle Placement there is a more direct approach, such as a cookery show endorsing a specific food brand.

3. **Influencers** - away from TV and film there are also celebrities who endorse products, such as wear certain brands of clothing. When a brand sends a celebrity items they are seeking Product Placement, often through paparazzi photos, social media or reviews.

Forms

Once a brand has established a relationship with an agency acting on their behalf, or in collaboration directly with a TV studio or film production company, placing the product can be found in the following formats:

- Logo within a scene
- Direct mention or usage
- Inclusion in plot
- Background placement
- Visible foreground placement

Understanding

Although more popular brands have larger networks and bigger budgets, smaller brands running Product Placement often notice soars in sales and overnight recognition. For example, a fashion brand that places their products in the hands of a well-known public figure is likely to see their popularity surge.

Example

Below is an example of Product Placement within a blockbuster film adaptation:

- **Yes Man and Ducati** - [43]The 2008 hit movie Yes Man starring Jim Carrey featured various product placements included Red Bull, UPS and Ducati. In one scene, the main character Carl rides a Ducati through the streets of Hollywood. The partnership fits with Ducati's brand of excitement and saying 'yes' to life.

Shared-Stores

Share-Store Partnerships are rapidly emerging on today's high-street. As retail competition grows, brands look to attract each other's customer base.

Definition

Where a partner provides agreed space within their own store for the other partner's brand. The primary brand has rented out, provided or extended their retail outlet to integrate the secondary brand.

Types

Shared-Store partnerships are becoming more common, and isn't just reserved for retail outlets, it can also be found online:

1. **Offline** - is the most common type of Shared-Store Partnership, where petrol stations, retail outlets, supermarkets and coffee shops have all been found to merge stores.

2. **Online** - a relatively new concept, but one that is increasing in popularity, brands combine areas of their websites together through iframing or creating dedicated sections.

Forms

Offline and online Shared-Store Partnerships can further be broken down into various forms:

Offline:

- **Store within a Store** - the classic form of a Shared-Store Partnership is to provide a section of the primary brand's retail space for another brand's store.

- **Promotional Area** - occasionally a store will offer some of their space as a promotional area to a partner brand, often manned by the partner brand's own personnel.

Online:

- **Dedicated Tab or Page** - providing a specific tab or page for a partner brand within the primary brand's website.

- **Members Area** - dedicated tabs or pages, but only for exclusive members, those under subscription services or rewarded to loyal consumers.

- **Iframing** - displaying a partner's webpage within your own website. Iframing acts as a window that shows a relevant section of their site within your own.

Understanding

Offline Shared-Stores places the partner brand physically in front of consumers within a store, allowing them to interact, touch and test a partner's product. Sharing retail space also minimises overall cost. Being alongside one another, both offline and online, creates a strong brand connection and attracts new consumers.

However, the risk for the primary brand is that they might be giving up an area of its store for another brand, which may end up not being as popular with their customers as they had hoped, or could even deter customers.

Example

We see Shared-Store partnerships every time we shop, with more and more retail outlets beginning to share their space to maximise options and attract customers, below is one such example:

- **Cineworld & Starbucks** - [44]Starbucks often use Shared-Store Partnerships to market their brand. In the UK, they selected the popular cinema chain Cineworld to host their store within the cinema's centres, aiming to attract new customers. [45]

Sponsorship

Sponsorship is a renowned marketing technique where well-known brands place their image alongside an event, team or project to create an association.

Definition

The marketing tactic of placing a brand alongside a particular event, displaying itself as a partner or supporter, with the objective to increase brand recognition and reputation.

Types

Sponsorship is one of the most successful ways to create a brand identity. Here are three types of Sponsorship:

1. **Awareness** - aligning a product alongside an event for mass exposure is the most common type of sponsorship. The aim is to have the largest possible reach.

2. **Association** - linking the product towards a cause, person or event to provide a brand association, so that every time the consumer thinks of that cause, person or event, they associate it with the sponsored brand.

3. **Consumer Understanding** – some brands are more complex than others, so sponsorship can be used to teach a consumer about what the product is offering.

Forms

Sponsorship comes in all shapes and sizes. Below are several varieties that are commonly found across many popular partnerships:

- **Sporting Sponsorships** - are some of the most expensive yet effective forms of brand exposure. They can be found within every popular sport from shirt sponsorships, stadium names and board advertisements.

- **Media Sponsorship** - any sponsorship found within TV, film and radio, such as the sponsoring of a television series.

- **Event Sponsorship** - sponsoring of events such as marathons, music festivals and concerts.

- **Local Sponsorship** - where small businesses use local events, such as farmers markets, fetes or political conventions to provide their brand exposure.

Understanding

Global brands such as Coca Cola, McDonalds and O2 spend millions of marketing spend on Sponsorships. Here are some of the main reasons why:

- Increases brand popularity
- Increases brand awareness
- Improves brand image
- Improves brand reputation
- Improves product understanding
- Utilised for product re-branding
- Drives traffic to product or website
- Reminds dormant customers to re-use products
- Opens new global or local markets

However, there can be some drawbacks:

- **Difficult to Track Performance** - noticing the increase in overall sales from a sponsorship is difficult as there is very little tracking in place, so companies can't tell exactly how many people saw their brand.

- **How to trigger Sales and Conversion** - at the end of the day brands must focus on sales, but sponsorship offers no clear call to action. Brand recognition is the main objective rather than direct sales.

Example

- **Barclays & English Premier League** - [46]Millions of pounds are spent on the English Premier Football League in the form of new player purchases, prize winnings and advertising. [47]Barclays, one of the UK's leading banks, is a long-standing sponsor of the Premier League. It capitalises on its global reach and millions of football followers.

4. Objectives & KPIs

What are the Partnership Objectives & KPIs?

Once a brand has decided which type of Partnership Marketing they wish to run, they must next consider what their aims and objectives are.

What are Objectives?

Objectives define what a brand wants to achieve as its overall outcome. This will be what the entire initiative is ultimately judged upon. Achieving it therefore depends on clear and measurable objectives.

Companies often use SMART objectives, making sure each objective has each of the following attributes:

- Specific
- Measurable
- Achievable
- Relevant
- Timely

What are KPIs?

Key Performance Indicators (KPIs) are used to quantify whether your objectives have been met.

Six Types of Objectives

The objectives used in Partnership Marketing are very similar to the ones used in general marketing. Here are the six main types of objectives:

1. New Customer Acquisition
2. Increase Customer Spend/Basket Size
3. Increase Customer Spend Frequency
4. Reactivation of dormant customers

5.   Improving Brand Awareness
6.   Generating Revenue through Advertising Commissions

The rest of this chapter will take a deeper look into each of these objectives and their relationship to the types of Partnership Marketing campaigns that can be run.

Partner Brand Objectives

When deciding on your objectives for a Partner Marketing campaign, you must also consider what your partner brand is aiming to achieve. Sometimes you will both be looking to achieve the same objective, but this may not always be the case. This differs from general marketing, as well as trying to complete your objectives, you must also work to achieve the partner brands aims too.

Example

Etihad Airways in Multi-Million Pound Manchester City Sponsorship

[48]Manchester City agreed the 10-year agreement worth £400million with the Abu Dhabi airline in 2009. The deal included sponsorship of the shirt, training kit and naming rights to the club's stadium and academy complex. The club's stadium was renamed the Etihad, forming the centre piece of a newly-named Etihad Campus, which makes up a large part of the Sport City site in East Manchester. Being partnered with such a successful club playing in the Barclays Premier League & UEFA Champions League gives Etihad Airways vast coverage to a global audience of sports fans.

This partnership involves many different objectives from both brands. Manchester City was looking to generate revenue from selling the sponsorship to Eithad, while also acquiring a whole host of new fans from the middle-east due to this connection. While Etihad was aiming to increase their brand image and acquire new customers from the Manchester City fan base and across the UK.

From *Abu Dhabi* to the world   FAQ | Contact us

Plan and book ▸ Etihad experience ▸ Before you fly ▸ Deals ▸ Destinations

Manchester City Football Club

Home > About us > Football > Manchester City Football Club

About the club

Etihad Airways has been Manchester City FC's main club partner since May 2009. During that time the club has enjoyed considerable success having picked up 4 trophies including 2 as the Barclays Premier League Champions.

Melbourne City Football Club
Click here to check out our sponsorship with Melbourne City FC.

The Club's stadium has been renamed as the Etihad Stadium, forming the center piece of a newly-named Etihad Campus, which encompasses a large part of the Sport City site in East Manchester.

Increasing New Customer Acquisition

Out of the six objectives most marketing campaigns focus on acquisition. Acquisition meaning the acquiring of new customers, is a fundamental marketing objective for most businesses.

<u>Objective</u>

The brands will be looking for access to each other's customer base in order to acquire new customers.

<u>Main KPIs</u>

An Acquisition Partnership Marketing campaign will often be judged upon the following KPIs:

- Number of new customers acquired

- Cost per acquisition (CPA)

- Lifetime value of acquired customers (LTV)

- Average revenue per user (ARPU)

- Conversion rates

With this objective the aim is to acquire as many customers as possible at the lowest possible cost. This means achieving the lowest cost per customer.

<u>Types of Partnerships</u>

These types of Partnership Marketing are most recommended when it comes to acquiring new customers:

- **Affiliation** - reaching out to your online affiliated partners to promote your product is a great way to acquire new customers. The advantages of this type over any other is that results are trackable.

- **Shared-Stores** - opening a store within a store is an interesting way to acquire new customers. By doing this the partner store will naturally bring in customers who will be drawn into your store.

- **Content** - joint content online is a growing acquisition technique. Savvy online brands are employing this to attract an audience interested in what both brands have to say.

Increasing Customer Spend/Basket Size

The second most popular objective is to encourage your existing customers to spend more. This is otherwise known as increasing their basket size.

Objective

Keeping existing customers happy year on year will be the sole driver to sustaining profits, rather than spending on continuous new acquisition. Here we are focusing on increasing customer basket size; the average amount a customer spends per visit or over the course of their lifecycle.

Main KPIs

A partnership focusing on increasing a customer's basket size is often measured using the following KPIs:

- Total spend per customer

- Average customer spend

- Lifetime value per customer (LTV)

To understand these you need to take a detailed look at your own customers, analysing their activity and breaking it down by customer segment.

Types of Partnerships

These types of Partnership Marketing are most successful at increasing customer spend:

- **Loyalty** - including exclusive partner offers in your loyalty programme encourages customers to spend more.

- **Sponsorship** - by increasing your exposure via sponsorship deals it can lead to improved popularity and recognisability. This encourages customers to repeat visit and spend more.

Increasing Customer Spend Frequency

Differing to the last objective, where the aim was to increase the customer's spend per purchase, the aim here is to increase how often a customer spends with you. Both objectives aim to increase the customers lifetime value.

Objective

A customer with greater spend frequency is worth far more than one-off purchasers. Brands that sell a product aim to increase the number of purchases, while a company that sells a service might look to increase the amount of time a customer uses them. Examples of this include Skype, or virtual games such as Pokémon Go, where they aim to increase the amount of time spent on their platform.

Main KPIs

The success of this objective can be analysed using the following KPIs:

- Total purchases made per customer

- Average number of purchases made per customer

- Average number of purchases made over a time period

- Lifetime value per customer

Types of Partnerships

These types of Partnership Marketing are most successful at increasing spend frequency:

- **Joint Product** - by creating a new joint product the chances are loyal customers will become even more engaged. This new product could be used as a reward with each purchase, which could lead to increased purchase frequency.

- **Distribution** - loyal customers will purchase more frequently if they can get their hands on it more often.

Reactivation of Dormant Customers

Overtime a customer's lifecycle will inevitably deplete. There are a whole host of factors in this, but they mainly depend on the type of product. The image below is an example of a typical customer lifecycle:

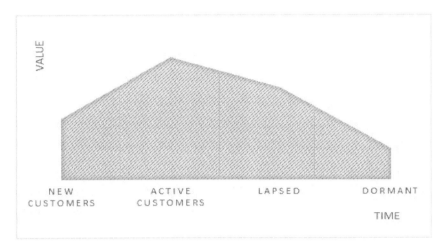

Dormancy is often described as any customer that has not made a purchase within a defined period; one week, one month or even one year, depending on your business, your customers segments and your products.

Objective

A customer that once used your product but no longer does is often of greater value than a new customer; they already understand the product which makes it less of an uphill task to re-educate them, and often all done at a lower cost than acquiring a new customer.

Fortunately, most brands today have such sophisticated CRM systems that they can easily detect when a customer drops into dormancy. And improvements in online communications, such as Email and Social Media, mean it is easier than ever before to get back in touch with customers.

Main KPIs

The success of this objective can be analysed using the following KPIs:

- Number of reactivated customers

- Number of new transactions made

- Value of new transactions

Types of Partnerships

These types of Partnership Marketing are most successful at reactivating dormant customers:

- **Sponsorship** - reminding a customer that your brand is still relevant and useful to them. Sponsorship can therefore remind a dormant customer of your presence.

- **Product Placement** - placing your product where old customers would see it, again reminding the customer of your product and your brand.

Improving Brand Awareness

When we see the logos of Coca Cola, Apple or Vodaphone, we know right away who they are and what they do. The more recognisable a brand, the better chance they have at being remembered and then purchased.

Objective

As an objective, brand awareness often raises debate. Huge companies plough vast sums of money into creating a strong, recognisable brand image, while many argue that it is probably better spent on digital marketing, which is trackable.

Main KPIs

Brand exposure is notoriously difficult to measure accurately, as it is predominantly offline, with no direct call to action (CTA). What can be looked at is the following:

- Number of visitors to an event where the brand is shown

- Number of new leads or sales during campaign period

- Increased website traffic during campaign period

If you know the number of people at an event where your brand is present, the number of people who saw your logo can be estimated, so you can add a Media Value per person. A Media Value is an industry agreed amount that each eye-ball on your logo is worth, which can give you an estimated ROI.

Types of Partnerships

These types of Partnership Marketing are most successful for improving brand awareness:

- **Sponsorship** - a popular way to gain brand exposure is for a company to sponsor an event. Sporting events, for example, provide huge opportunities for brands to be placed in front of mass TV audiences.

- **Charitable** - working with charity events is an excellent way for firms to receive positive PR, exposure and brand mentions.

Generating Revenue through Advertising Commissions

Brands can decide to sell advertising space to partners on their own website, product or within their stores. Those that do, find it advantageous in terms of revenue earned.

The downside is the perception of 'selling out', they do not wish to cannibalise their own sites by advertising partner offers in such a way.

Objective

Online this objective is often achieved by giving-up some of your website as ad-space. This can come in the form of individual ad-spots, promotional areas or separate minisite's. Offline a brand can provide advertising on their packaging or within their stores.

Main KPIs

Measuring advertising revenue all comes down to tracking. If sufficient tracking is in place the following metrics can be calculated:

- Number of banner clicks or views

- Conversion of clicks/views to sales

- Revenue generated

- Increasing LTV

These metrics can help you determine whether selling your ad space has been advantageous to your brand.

Types of Partnerships

Below are examples of the types of Partnership Marketing best used to earn revenue through advertising:

- **Affiliation** - rather than working with partners to promote yourselves in the traditional partnership model, here the roles have reversed where you are the one promoting them via your ad-space.
- **Loyalty** - creates an excellent opportunity to raise revenue by selling off space in your loyalty programme. Here brands can charge partners to feature.

Examples of Campaign Objectives

Acquiring Customers: Starbucks and New Look join forces

[49]New Look is one of the leading UK clothes retailers. Starbucks is one the world's leading coffee shop brands featuring on almost every high street.

Here they partnered via a Shared-store agreement, to offer customers the option to sit down, have a coffee, and relax during their shopping experience. This is a niche feature that allows both retail outlets to be present under one roof.

This set up not only keeps existing customers in the store for longer, but it also attracts new ones. For New Look specifically it means loyal Starbucks customers are more inclined to enter, whereas Starbucks gain new customers from browsing shoppers.

Brand Awareness: American Express sponsorship

[50]American Express often run sponsorship campaigns for brand awareness, and by partnering with the Summer Series Music Festival,

situated at London's Somerset House, arranged by the Bigfish music partnership agency, they looked to gain exposure to the young, trendy and affluent audience.

By linking their brand to the festival, they found that 70% of attendees were more aware of the American Express brand and 20% shared a selfie with the hashtag #Amexsounds. This shows the power of sponsorship and the recognition that it brings.

Ad Space Revenue Generation: PayPal Minisite

[51]PayPal is an American company founded in 1998 and is one of the most recognised online payment options in the world. Their online wallet serves as an electronic alternative to debit and credit card.

With millions of users, they actively partake in Partnership Marketing. They do this mainly by providing ad-space on their Offers Ministe to their merchants, often in return for commissions, or improved exposure on the partner's side.

Here they offer exclusive PayPal only offers to entice their customers to click through and uptake the partner brands offer. They work closely with each and every partner to arrange the offers, negotiate the ad-placements, and look to benefit in terms of commissions, as well as an improved consumer experience. [52]

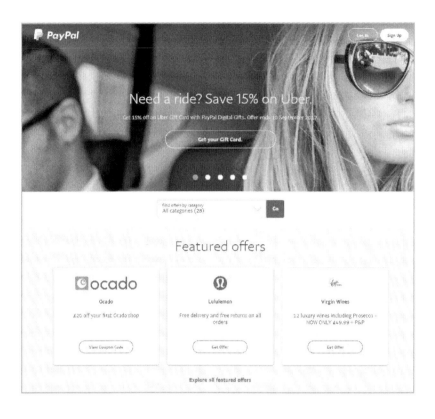

5. Utilising Assets

What are Partnership Marketing Assets?

Once you know what objectives you are aiming for, the next step is to determine where you will be promoting a partner to your customers. These promotional areas are called assets.

What are Assets?

An asset is anywhere that a primary brand will provide exposure for a secondary one, otherwise known as inventory. Online it can also be referred to as Owned Media, the content or properties of your site that you own.

Common Examples

In today's ever-evolving marketing, the number of assets a brand can use is always growing and changing, examples include:

- Promotional minisite

- Product packaging

- Newsletter feature

- Advertorial or editorial

- Skyscraper, MPU or leaderboard banner ad placements

- In-store promotional stand

- Iframing webpage

- Social media posts and tweets

- Blog post or mention

- Sponsorship on stadiums, merchandise or products

- Whitepapers

As you can see assets come in all shapes and sizes, from an advert in a brand's newsletter, to sponsorship on an entire stadium. The assets offered to a secondary brand will be dependent on the marketing channels the primary brand has available.

Example

Secret Escapes promote Hunter's in Newsletter

[53]Secret Escapes is fast emerging as the travel booking site of choice for many consumers looking for luxurious and classy holiday destinations and packages. They are earning the reputation as the go-to website for travel enthusiasts looking for something high-end and unique.

[54]Hunters Boots was founded in 1856, their long-standing brand resonates class and upmarket. Their boots are a becoming more renowned and famous, seen across muddy summer festivals up and down the UK.

These two companies share customer audiences, they are both adventurous, high-end, and expensive. In this partnership Secret Escapes have utilised their asset, their newsletter, to feature Hunters Boots. They sent this newsletter to a specific customer segment with high open-rates. This shows how a simple asset such as a newsletter can be highly effective and promoting a partner.

The promotion consisted of an exclusive offer to Secret Escapes customers, using a CouponCode HUNTERESCAPE10. The newsletter tied in words like adventure, outdoors and escape, which bring the two brands together to engage the common audience.

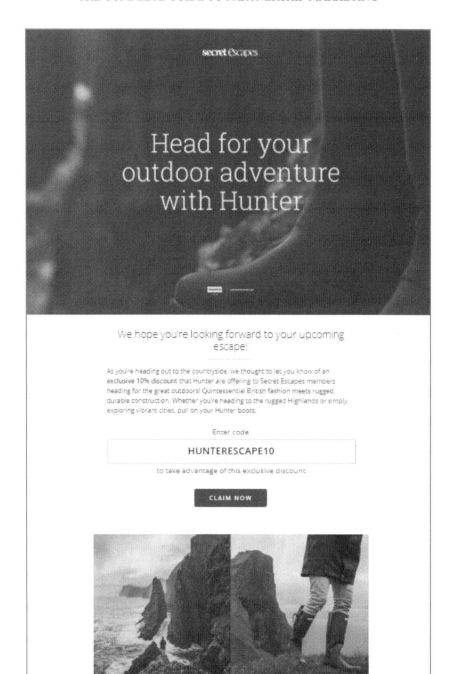

Auditing your Assets

A primary brand must decide which of their assets they will offer to which partners. The most organised method of doing so is to document all possible assets, then create a schedule in which to manage them.

What is an audit?

An audit is an entire overview of all areas that a primary brand has to offer a secondary brand for exposure, a complete record of all possible assets. Experienced Partnership Marketing teams tend to organise this using spreadsheet, outlining what collateral they have available, whether it be on-site, instore, product or event related.

Creating the Asset Audit

The best way of constructing an asset audit is to slice it by marketing channel, listing these in one column, while in the second column listing the specific assets you could offer for each channel. Here's an example:

Channel	Asset
Onsite	Homepage Display Ad Space
	Blog Page Header Ad Space
	On-site calculator sponsorship
	Footer placement
	Log-out pop up placement
	Advertorial Blog Post
Email	Solus Email
	Feature in VIP Monthly
	Feature in Reactivation Weekly
	Half page in Loyalty Scheme Email
	Feature in Transactional Email footer
Social	Dedicated Facebook Friday Post
	Twitter Header Takeover
	Daily Pinterest Post
Sponsorship	Sponsorship of Competition Page
	Logo at Summer Charity Event

You should list everything you can think of and continuously update it as your assets evolve and you work with more partners. To create a very accurate audit it takes a strong understanding of the entire business, every marketing channel, as well as product roadmaps. A strong relationship with all stakeholders really helps too, this includes email marketing and social media teams, website owners and product developers, all of which will assist in your audit creation and guide you on what is possible and available, and where you could include a partner brand.

Asset Decisions

Once the audit has been created, you next need to decide which of the assets you can offer to your partner. This can be decided in several ways:

- **Request from Partner** - often a partner will come to you asking to be promoted to your customer base, they may also request a specific position to be promoted in. You can take your asset audit and allocate a specific position to your partner.

- **Availability** - a simple way to decide which assets to allocate is to simply give a partner what is available at the time. You might be working with many partners and therefore only have limited availability at certain times (more on how to manage this in the next section).

- **The Customer** - the recommend way to decide is based on what is most relevant to the customer and the customer journey. If there is an asset in a specific part of your website which will be most effective at engaging your audience, then this is the one to offer to a partner brand.

- **Conversion Rates** - some brands prefer to be more scientific with their choice and allocate positions based on their customer data. They will provide positions to certain partners based on the conversion rate. For example, you may decide to promote a specific partner in your newsletters as you know it will convert at a certain rate, compared to perhaps a mention in your social media feed.

- **Highest Value** - another way is to provide a position based on monetary value. You can select an asset to give a partner based on how much it is worth, giving away a position at the highest value to receive a high value asset on their end in return.

Expanding your Asset Audit

Considering the points above, to assist further in your decision-making process, you can expand your Asset Audit and list the conversion rates and monetary value of each position. Here is how that could look:

Channel	Asset	Av.Conversion Rate	Value (per month)
Onsite	Homepage Display Ad Space	5.00%	£ 5,000
	Blog Page Header Ad Space	5.50%	£ 3,000
	On-site calculator sponsorship	7.50%	£ 2,000
	Footer placement	7.75%	£ 2,000
	Log-out pop up placement	9.00%	£ 3,000
	Advertorial Blog Post	2.00%	£ 1,000
Email	Solus Email	4.70%	£ 6,000
	Feature in VIP Monthly	2.60%	£ 2,000
	Feature in Reactivation Weekly	5.90%	£ 3,000
	Feature in Active Update	6.60%	£ 1,000
	Half page in Loyalty Scheme Email	0.70%	£ 750
	Feature in Transactional Email footer	5.67%	£ 500
Social	Dedicated Facebook Friday Post	4.30%	£ 350
	Twitter Header Takeover	2.10%	£ 750
	Daily Pinterest Post	1.00%	£ 500
Sponsorship	Sponsorship of Competition Page	3.40%	£ 2,000
	Logo at Summer Charity Event	0.90%	£ 1,000

With this, now you can filter and rank accordingly, so when it comes to choosing which asset to allocate, you can make a decision that is right for both your brand and the partner brand.

Managing your Assets

As mentioned, you might be working with multiple partner brands across multiple assets, which needs to be organised effectively. There are several options to organise your assets; firstly, you can simply take your Asset Audit and expand it to include dates per asset, and it'll look like this:

Channel	Asset	Av.Conversion Rate	Value (per month)	Dates
Onsite	Homepage Display Ad Space	5.00%	£ 5,000	8th May
	Blog Page Header Ad Space	5.50%	£ 3,000	
	On-site calculator sponsorship	7.50%	£ 2,000	
	Footer placement	7.75%	£ 2,000	10th May
	Log-out pop up placement	9.00%	£ 3,000	8th May
	Advertorial Blog Post	2.00%	£ 1,000	
Email	Solus Email	4.70%	£ 6,000	12th May
	Feature in VIP Monthly	2.60%	£ 2,000	
	Feature in Reactivation Weekly	5.90%	£ 3,000	8th May
	Feature in Active Update	6.60%	£ 1,000	
	Half page in Loyalty Scheme Email	0.70%	£ 750	
	Feature in Transactional Email footer	5.67%	£ 500	
Social	Dedicated Facebook Friday Post	4.30%	£ 350	10th May
	Twitter Header Takeover	2.10%	£ 750	
	Daily Pinterest Post	1.00%	£ 500	
Sponsorship	Sponsorship of Competition Page	3.40%	£ 2,000	12th May
	Logo at Summer Charity Event	0.90%	£ 1,000	

This is an example partnering with UK supermarket, Tesco. Here you have allocated them three assets on the 8th May, two on the 10th May and two on the 12th May. For each brand you work with you can create a new table.

The Asset Calendar

Alternatively, you can create an Asset Calendar. This lists the dates and which partners are allocated to which positions. It looks like this:

January	Asset	Partner	Price	Exchange	Forecast
1st					
2nd	Homepage Ad Space	Boots			
3rd	Homepage Ad Space	Boots			
4th	Homepage Ad Space	Boots			
5th					
6th	Inactive Newsletter	Coca Cola			
7th					

8th	Display Campaign	PayPal			
9th	Blog Post	Tesco			
10th					
11th	Twitter Post	Lonely Planet			

This format allows you to include a column for the exchange of exposure you might be receiving in return, and the forecast of the campaign (more on how to do this later). This also gives you the option to have the Asset Calendar as a separate working document to the Asset Audit, using it to manage your day to day asset allocation.

The Asset Portfolio

An Asset or Inventory Portfolio is a graphic representation of your assets on offer. This is a useful document to illustrate to a partner what you can offer and can come in many shapes and sizes:

- **PowerPoint Presentation** - the most common way to display a portfolio, using the one slide per asset rule.

- **Manual** - describes all available assets, often made using Microsoft Word, more text heavy than a PowerPoint deck.

- **One Pager** - one pager that bullet points the available assets.

- **Infographic** - illustrated one pager.

PowerPoint Example

The purpose of an Asset Portfolio is to sell your brand to prospecting partners and highlight the advantages of each asset. It is important to clearly highlight conversion rates, prices and sizes. Here is an example of some of the main slides to include:

Introduction

A typical portfolio begins with an initial slide describing your brand, your customer base and types of segments. This gives partners a useful understanding of who you are and what you have to offer.

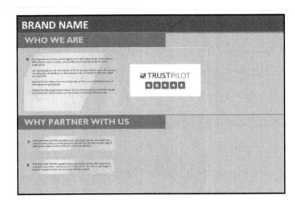

Newsletters

This slide describes your newsletter assets and it's benefits. It should have effective imagery alongside information on recipient volumes and banner sizes.

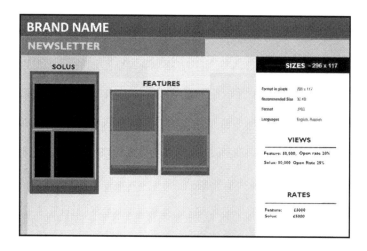

Homepage Exposure

One of the most valuable assets is one's website homepage. Providing exposure on a page that commonly receives the highest monthly views is extremely sought after. Here the portfolio highlights the key advertising spots available, also making it clear what materials are required.

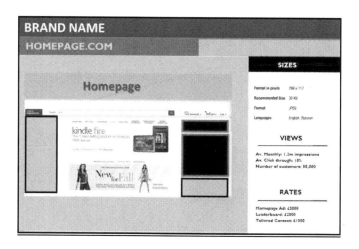

Digital One Pager Example

Rather than a PowerPoint or print out version, I've seen some brands embrace the digital age and create an interactive digital one pager. This is an example from The Mail Online who openly encourage potential partners to browse all of their available assets, and view sizes and requirements, all on one page:

http://mailonlinecreative.co.uk/specs/#leaderboard

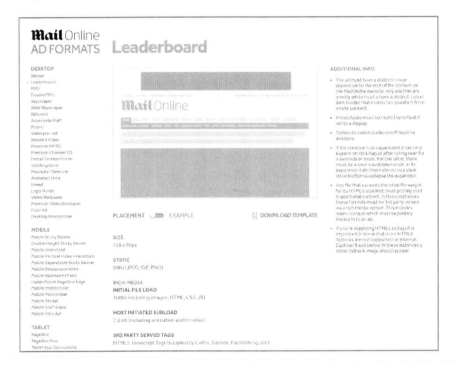

To Exchange or Sell your Assets

An important stage in the asset allocation is to define commercial terms. What are you going to give your assets away for? There are generally two approaches:

1. **Exchange Campaigns** - partners agree to promote each other in return for exposure on the opposing partner's side.

2. **Paid-for Campaigns** - the primary brand offers their marketing assets to a secondary brand in return for payment.

To Exchange or Sell?

The decision of whether to exchange or sell often comes down to the situation and the partner. If the partner doesn't offer equal exposure on their end then the decision has been made for you, it must be sold instead. While some partners simply won't work with you unless you exchange assets. However, some partnerships may use a combination of the two. It all depends on what the partner is willing to agree.

Negotiation

When it comes to agreeing whether to exchange or pay, there is likely to be a negotiation phase. This is the commercial end of the partnership and both sides will want to achieve the best deal possible.

Tips here are to be cooperative, transparent and flexible. The aim is to agree, not to out-do one another. You should always aim to bring the conversation back to ROI. As long as the exchange of assets offered, or the agreed price of sale, provides the right return for both sides, then the negotiation process should be very smooth.

Examples of Utilising your Online Assets

Barclaycard promote Uber onsite and via newsletters

[55]Barclaycard is a multinational credit card and payment services provider, and a division of Barclays plc. [56]Uber has taken the taxi service industry by storm and runs the world's most popular taxi booking app, they also have services such as UberEats.

Barclaycard has decided to utilise its own site in this example to feature Uber. Here they have offered a specific promotional area onsite for Uber directed at existing customers. They also send newsletters and direct mail out to customers to promote Uber. Uber in return are offering an exclusive offer to Barclaycard users where every 11th trip gets up to £15 discount.

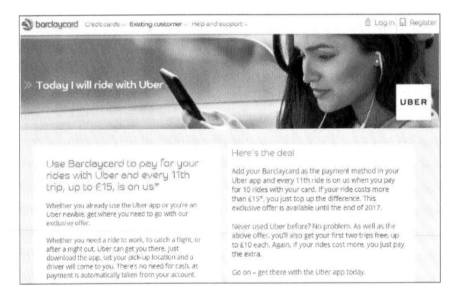

EasyJet integrate Booking.com onsite

[57]EasyJet is a British airline carrier serving Europe with its low-cost all-economy flights. Founded in 1995 it is the largest airline of the United Kingdom by number of passengers carried.

[58]Founded in 1996 Booking.com is now one of the most popular accommodation booking sites in the world. Based in Amsterdam they currently attract over 30 million unique visitors a month.

[59]In 2012 both brands forged a very innovative partnership. EasyJet decided to move away from its existing online accommodation provider Laterooms.com to Booking.com to expand its offering.

They integrated Booking.com as a permanent platform for all users seeking a hotel room. Here EasyJet have used their Hotels section of their site as an asset to Booking.com.

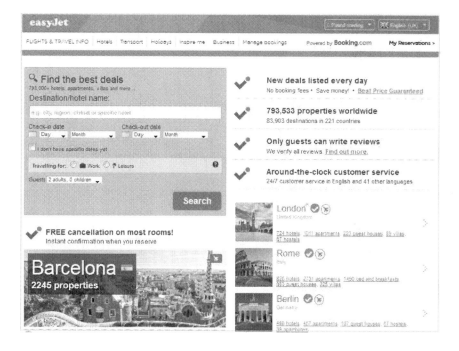

EasyJet offer Europcar in exclusive online exposure

Along with Booking.com, [60]EasyJet also collaborate with Europcar in a very similar way, offering exclusive car rental deals to their customers. Europcar is one of the leading car rental companies in Europe.

EasyJet again leverage their site to iframe Europcar's webpage, integrating it into the EasyJet site. Here users can search as they would on the Europcar site for car rentals without leaving the EasyJet site.

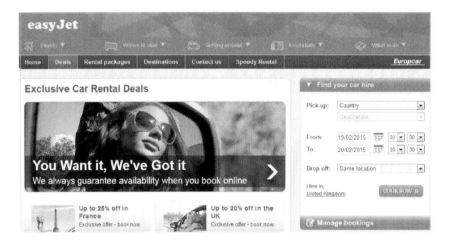

6. Deciding your Partners

What is a Partner?

Fundamental to Partnership Marketing is finding the right partner. This chapter takes an in-depth look into the types of partners, and how to locate, manage and get the best out of them.

Definition

A partner is any company that is willing to promote your products or services to their target audience, and therefore work with you on marketing partnerships.

Types of partner

There are partners who seek long term relationships, spanning years or decades, while others seek much shorter partnerships, such as just for a day or a week. Success isn't dependent on the length of the partnership; sometimes very quick partnerships can be the most effective.

Every brand has the option to partner up, regardless of their size. Some large companies, as we have already shown, team up with other large brands. However, some focus on smaller partners, depending on the situation.

Large or Small Partners

There are advantages of partnering with both large and small companies, the decision eventually comes down to the objectives and strategy at hand.

Larger Brands

- Greater resources
- Mass Appeal
- Wide Network and Reach
- Established Reputation

- Range of Customer Segments
- Experience

Smaller Brands

- Flexibility and Freedom
- Product Adaptability
- Less direct contacts to work with
- Quicker to organise a campaign
- Better chance of an undamaged past reputation

Examples

Spotify and Genius make the perfect partnership

[61]Founded in 2008, Spotify is one of the leading music streaming services in the world, providing users access to millions of songs and thousands of artists. [62]Founded in 2009, Genius is a less well-known digital media company, predominantly focusing on providing lyrics and stories behind the music.

In 2016 Spotify decided to partner up with Genius to provide their users with interesting anecdotes, stories and lyrics behind some of their most popular streamed songs. This addition aimed to set Spotify apart from their competitors by giving something extra to their customers, something they believed the consumers would want and would benefit their experience with the app.

The partnership was a huge success, with Spotify integrating the service initially from just one genre of music as a trial, to every mainstream song on the app.

This shows that big and small companies can team up successfully. Genius' reputation and popularity soured by teaming up with one of the biggest brand names in the world. On the other hand, Spotify benefited by integrating a niche service to set themselves apart from competitors, and add value to their product.

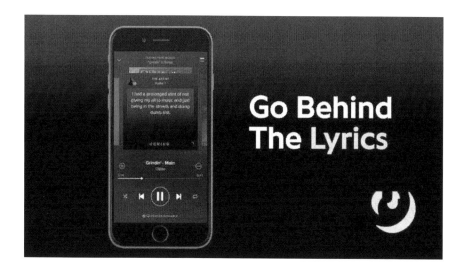

Travel at a discount with Virgin Trains and Festival No6

[63]Virgin Trains is a train operating company owned by Virgin and Stagecoach. They are known as one of the leading train lines in the UK, operating popular cross-country routes.

Festival N°6 is an annual art and music festival held in Portmeirion, Wales. The festival presents a wide range of music genres including folk, house and dance.

Virgin Trains partnered with the popular festival as their exclusive travel partner, to capitalise on the influx of people heading out to the festive, and offering attendees advanced tickets at 25% discount.

This partnership promoted Virgin to all festival goers as the transportation of choice. For Festival N°6 this partnership provided expansive customer reach via Virgin's communication channels and exclusive online content, as shown below.

Virgin trains
arrive AWESOME
FESTIVAL Nº6
PORTMEIRION
EXPERIENCE A JOURNEY UNLIKE
Any Other
- TO A FESTIVAL LIKE NO OTHER -
We're back as the official Travel Partner of Festival No.6 - a festival like no other, in stunning Portmeirion, North Wales from 3 - 6 September 2015.
With a line-up including Belle & Sebastian, Grace Jones, Metronomy, James, Catfish & The Bottlemen, Years & Years, Mark Ronson, Irvine Welsh, and much much more. Festival No.6 boasts an eclectic selection of the best in music, arts, culture and food. Like the sound of this? Book your festival tickets here.
Arrive at the festival in speed, comfort and style, with some special touches thrown in for good measure. We'll also give you an exclusive 25% off Advance fares to Bangor (the closest station to Festival No.6) when you travel with us.
BOOK TICKETS NOW »
OFFICIAL TRAVEL PARTNER
Virgin trains
25% OFF ADVANCE FARES

Identifying Current Partners

Most companies collaborate in some shape or form. This isn't always a marketing collaboration, as their partners could also be business relationships such as suppliers or agencies.

Therefore, the first step to identifying who to partner with, from a marketing perspective, is to understand who your company already has a relationship with. A suggested technique is to record your company's internal network by creating a Partner Map.

<u>Creating a Partner Map</u>

Anyone already familiar with Mind-Maps will recognise it. Before piecing it together you will need to gather the relevant information to populate it. The first step is to speak to your company's internal teams.

The first team to approach is Procurement as they hold all contractual agreements with partners, mainly suppliers. They should be able to supply you with company names that you are working with and in what capacity.

Next, speak with every internal department to learn about their external relationships, and add those to the Map. This includes Accounting, Legal, HR, Operations and Marketing. Ask your colleagues in each department who they work with, what suppliers do they use, what software do they rent, what agencies do they employ, and what companies do they speak to.

Once you have located all existing relationships, add these to the map by splitting the map into relationship categories. When the map has been fully populated, you should colour-code each department for a clearer view. Here is an example:

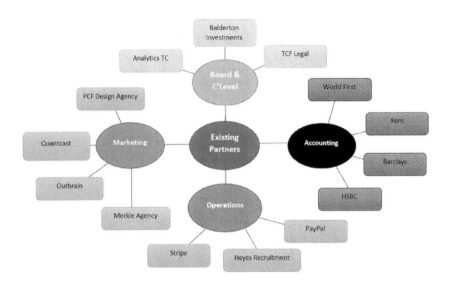

Locating New Partners

Now that existing relationships have been mapped, how can you locate new ones? Whether online or offline, there are several options to identify them.

Online

This exercise essentially encourages you to get researching. Starting online, research your brand. Search your popular keywords, recording the companies which appear, particularly those also bidding on your keywords. Look at your competitors and who they are affiliated with. Read articles where your company is mentioned, taking note of any other companies mentioned. Seek out agencies that specialise in your industry and record who they work with. If you are already using a marketing agency, reach out to them to share their network.

Social Media is another way to research new partners. LinkedIn offers the most powerful networking tool, suggesting new contacts from related companies. It also gives you the profiles of your Partnership Marketing counterparts. Twitter and Facebook are also useful, particularly brands that are actively advertising there.

Offline

Away from your laptop there are more traditional methods. Reach out and ask your own suppliers for introductions and names. Use your own knowledge of the industry, it should not be underestimated, and jot down your ideas, previous companies you worked for and brands you like or use. Ask friends or family who they think might be relevant, and visit stores to see which brands are placed alongside one another or that customers tend to purchase together.

Also make sure to get out to roadshows or industry events. In the gambling industry, for example, the main event each year is [64]ICE, where hundreds of brands exhibit. PerformanceIN and IAB also hold annual events full of likeminded companies. These events are a hot-bed for networkers and new partnerships, so a great chance to speak with your counterparts, forging relationships and inquiring about collaboration.

Partnership Contact Page

Another option is to allow new partners to come to you. Have a sign-up page on your website for all those who express an interest in working with you. There are two ways this can be done; firstly, the page can simply be a 'contact us' page with your email address on, such as this example of the page I used while working at Nutmeg.com:

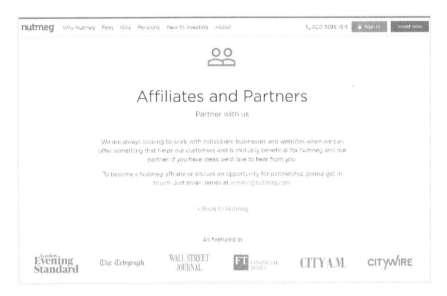

Or the page can ask potential partners to complete a Partnership Application form. This can be a downloadable PDF to gather all information you wish to know about a potential partner; what type of collaboration are they seeking, their reach and assets on offer. From here you may select those perceived to be the right fit for your brand. For example:

Name:	
Contact email:	
Address:	

Brand name:	
Asset Request:	
Dates/Period Requested:	
Conversion Estimates:	
Promotion description:	

Partnership Portal

Lastly, some companies take the contacts page a step further and allow brands to actively take their creatives from the offset, download guidelines and request new content.

In many ways it works just like an affiliate program does, where you create an account that allows you full access to their marketing suite. Here is an example from [65]Netflix who have a complete portal for partners:

Expanding the Partner Map

When companies start to get in touch, you can add these to your Partner Map. You can begin to colour code new partners against existing ones. You could also highlight separately those with the most potential, and those less suitable for collaboration.

In the below example, existing partners are labelled grey and potential new partners in light-orange. Further sub-categorisation has also been done with internal relationship categories marked in orange circles, while external relationship categories in black circles.

Contact details have also been added, while job descriptions and LinkedIn profiles of your counterparts at these companies can also been included to give you a complete picture of your partnership network.

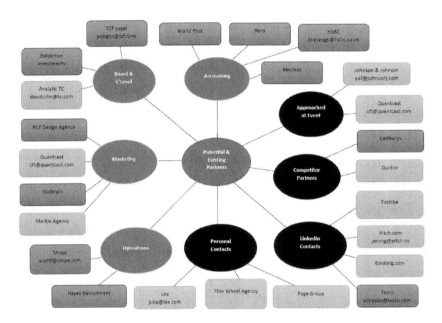

Establishing whether a partner is the right fit

<u>The 10 Factors</u>

Now your entire network is visible, it is important to decide which potential partners are the right fit for your business. There are 10 factors to determine this, they should separate the perfect partners from the 'maybes':

1. **Target Audience** - the most successful partnerships are when two brands have similar target audiences and common customer profiles across segments. Using one of our previous examples, EasyJet and Booking.com have very similar audiences; the traveller.

2. **Brand Recognition & Reputation** - a brand that is easily recognisable, has a high NPS (net-promoter-score) with both customers and employees, and with a trustworthy reputation is a key factor.

3. **Location** - a partner's location is a consideration if you want to work with someone local to you. However, with our ever-improving communication technologies this may not be an issue.

4. **Markets** - it is best to run with a partner whose strongest markets match your own. If your brand is large in the UK and Germany then teaming up with one that is big in Asia may not make much sense, unless of course you plan to enter the Asian market.

5. **Resources** - the technical resources and personnel that a partner has should be similar to that of your company.

6. **Partnership History** - if a brand has multiple proven partnership successes then collaboration is a no-brainer. You may wish to reconsider a brand which lacks experience or a has been unsuccessful in the past.

7. **Growth** - are they profitable and is their market share increasing? Are they dominating against competitors? A growing partner is one you can potentially jump on the bandwagon with.

8. **Company Size** - small firms with a strong reputation as a niche and technical brand might be the best fit over a larger establishment. While a larger brand is far more recognisable and might have greater impact.

9. **Available Assets** - are the assets a partner can promote you with appealing? Will they reach their customers? What they can offer you is a big decision maker.

10. **Price Offered** - if they are paying you, who's offering the highest price?

You should not base your decisions on just one of these factors, each of the above should be considered to ensure you make the right decision for your company.

Right-fit Brands

After using the Partner Map and considering the 10 factors, at the end of the process you will have chosen what are referred to as 'Right-fit' brands.

This means the right partner is one your customers will be comfortable with, engage and purchase from. It also means they have the right products for your customers, a respected brand image and similar customers to your own.

Examples

Win an Aston Martin with PokerStars.com

[66]PokerStars is the largest online poker room in the world, providing millions of users the platform to play poker twenty-four-seven. In 2012 they bought out their closest competitors, Full Tilt, to become the undisputed online poker brand.

Aston Martin Limited is a British manufacturer of luxury sports cars. They are a stand out name alongside Ferrari, Lamborghini and Porsche in the industry.

The long-standing partnership involves both brands collaborating in a number of ways including an Aston Martin car show at the World Series of Poker hosted by PokerStars, the sponsorship of the Aston Martin Speed racing cars, and the opportunity to win the car at PokerStars tournaments.

The two brands are extremely like-minded; they share the same target audience, the high-rolling poker player who enjoys a luxury lifestyle, have high brand recognition, operating in similar market, with comparable company size and resources available.

Pass Go and win with the McDonalds and Monopoly Partnership

[67]In 2015 McDonalds and Monopoly, celebrated their 10th year as annual partners. The partnership involves a Monopoly-styled game in McDonald's restaurants, giving customers the chance to win high profile prizes. There are also further collaborations when it comes to the prizes, including EasyJet, Samsung and boohoo.com.

Both brands have the right reputation, recognisability and history to suit each other. Both brands are similar as they have a long history of mass-market loyal customers. For McDonalds it is a great match as it allows them to use a well-known brand to reward customers with prizes, and for Monopoly it promotes their game to a new generation of players.

The Importance of Target Audience Similarity

Out of the ten factors there are two that really stand out, the target audience and brand reputation. If a partner doesn't fit either of these, it's best to not consider them any further. Firstly, let's take a closer look at the target audience and why this is such a key decision maker.

Customer Profiling

Who are your customers? Observing a brand's audience, you will notice they consists of many different segments, each with different profiles. Customer Profiling means understanding the key characteristics of these segments to create a description for each type of customer. The most common characteristics described are:

- Age range
- Demographic
- Location
- Personal Interests
- Spending Habits
- Income
- Lifestyle

To create Customer Profiles, you can undertake data-led research, focus groups or online surveys to learn who your customers are and their typical traits. Doing this activity creates a better understanding of your customers and how to meet their needs.

Does your Target Audience Resonate with the Partner?

The reason why profiling your customers is so important for Partnership Marketing, is that it will allow you to understand if your customers are similar to theirs. If they are alike, they are far more likely to engage with the partner brand and the promotion.

At my time working at Nutmeg, it was important for us to understand who are customers were, as we would only work with other companies where they had similar customers, and so would likely be interested in what Nutmeg has to offer.

To understand if your partner does have the right audience for you ask them some of the following questions:

- Can you outline your customer's interests, needs and wants?
- What is their lifecycle in terms of loyalty and reactivation?
- What is the average spend frequency and basket size?
- Where did your customers hear about you or join from?
- Have your customers engaged with partner offers before?
- What are the conversion rates on your marketing campaigns?

Example

Audience Similarity from GQ Magazine and Wilkinson Sword

[68]GQ is an international lifestyle magazine. The publication focuses on men's fashion and culture.[69]UK based Wilkinson Sword started as a sword, motorcycle and gardening tools brand, now more widely known for razor blades.

GQ agreed to host a dedicated section of their site for Wilkinson Sword, including reviews, shaving guides and competitions. The two brands are an example of how important it is to have similar target audiences. Both customers contain similar traits of age, gender, disposable income and lifestyle. It's because of this the two are long standing partners, working together predominantly in Content Partnership Marketing. [70]

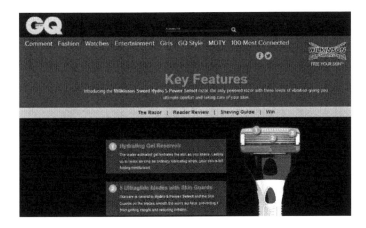

The Importance of Brand Recognition & Reputation

Equally important to audience similarity is Brand Recognition and Reputation. Customers will only be engaged if they understand or recognise the partner brand.

A Brand's Image

What is a brand's image? It can reference anything that ties into the companies' perception and proposition. A brand's image should include all the following elements:

- Company Logo
- Unique Product Features
- Company Culture and Values
- Company Reputation
- Company History
- Advertising
- Tone of Voice

A powerful image can deliver emotional association, where customers feel loyal to a brand. Branding also refers to company personality and how a brand speaks and acts.

Analysing Their Image

Distinguishing whether a brand's image will resonate with your audience can be examined through five areas:

1. **Recognisability** - do your customers know who they are?

2. **Pulling Power** - will customers be drawn to the brand and the offer?

3. **PR Enhancement** - is the brand strong enough to improve your own reputation? And can you utilise this through PR?

4. **Trust & Values** - does the partner brand have similar ethics that will resonate with your own audience?

5. **Historic Reputation** - has the partner ever been involved in unethical practices or ran campaigns that would not support your image? Its best to avoid such brands whose reputation was once poor.

Analysing these will provide a good understanding to whether a brand's image will fit. If they tick many of the boxes, then they should resonate well with your audience.

Example

Red Bull and GoPro partnership is out of this world

[71]Red Bull is an Austrian manufactured energy drink created in 1987. Their brand image is distinguished by their well-known slogan 'gives you wings' and their sponsorship activities aim to support that.

The 2012 event named The Stratos, in which Felix Baumgartner, an Austrian skydiver, jumped to earth from a helium balloon, breaking the vertical freefall distance world record. It was sponsored and partly funded by Red Bull and watched by millions around the world. The stunt was also in partnership with portable camera brand GoPro. GoPro placed their product on the helmet of Baumgartner to capture the event live for us all to witness.

The stunt produced fantastic exposure for Red Bull and illustrated the GoPro in its finest light. The reason it worked so well is because the two big brand names came together, both with strong brand recognition relating to adventure and exhilaration. This shows the power of such a marketing partnership and importance of tying in your brand with the right partners for maximum effect.

Examples of Audience and Brand Match

TripAdvisor add value with Deliveroo

[72]In July 2017 TripAdvisor, one of the world's most popular travel and restaurant review app, announced the integration of Deliveroo, leading food delivery service, into their content. This partnership connects 20,000 restaurants with the option to order Deliveroo from within the app.

This is an example of two brands with a similar target audience, the gastronome, and strong brand reputation teaming up. It also shows how a content site can monetise with the use of a partner brand, earning off each Deliveroo order. It is dynamic, slick and adds value to the customer.

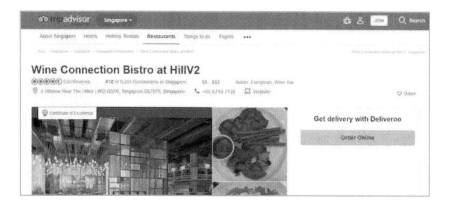

TripAdvisor in partnership with Opentable

Secondly, TripAdvisor has a similar relationship with Opentable. The restaurant reservation website is also integrated into the TripAdvisor content, so customers can easily book a table at their favourite restaurants without ever having to leave the TripAdvisor platform. Again, this resonates with the audience, adds value and benefits both parties.

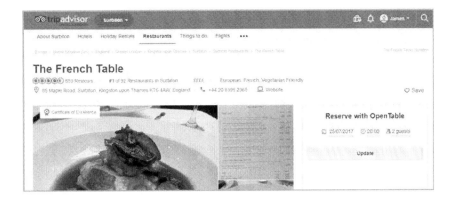

7. Partner Relations

Forging a Strong Relationship

Once a decision has been made on which partners you are going to work with, you now want to establish strong relationships with each. One of the main aspects to forging a strong partnership is to have a solid relationship with your Partnership Marketing counterpart.

<u>Counterpart</u>

It is important that you and your Partnership Marketing counterpart have the following personal traits if the partnership between your companies is going to be a success:

- Honesty
- Availability
- Mutual Respect
- Integrity
- Understanding

If both sides want it to be a long-lasting relationship, then these should be the backbone of all communications and campaign planning.

<u>Communications</u>

Communications between one another will define the partnership. Being honest and open is important, but it also matters how you speak to one another, the tone used, and how often.

Communication techniques are taught to top salespeople and account managers at most companies, and the same skills apply here for Partnership Marketing personnel. Tone of voice, and efficiency of conversations at each stage of the campaign process matter a great deal. Keeping the tone professional reminds the partner you are proficient, while friendless portrays willingness to cooperate in an open manner. An understanding of their business, knowing their customers, their brand values and their end objectives all matter. Mutual respect, being hospitable, and speaking on equal terms, should all lead to a very successful partnership.

Negotiating the Campaign Elements

Once objectives and assets have been agreed with a partner, next comes deciding the campaign specifics. This means agreeing on all elements that piece together the campaign. The main ones to consider are:

- What offer will be shown?
- How many customers will be targeted?
- What price will be paid, when and how?
- What type of tracking is required?
- Which channels will be used?
- How long will the campaign last?
- What banner sizes, packaging or in-store stands are required?

Deciding these will define the core elements of the campaign. At this stage they should be discussed, negotiated and agreed upon, so that a clear picture starts to take place of how the partnership campaign will work.

Timings

Timings are a crucial factor in all of this. Partners should discuss openly when certain actions will need to happen. There will be a matter of negotiation as partners discuss whose resources will be used, but eventually an agreement on what needs to be produced, and for when, will be met.

Setting Expectations

When it comes to negotiating anything with a partner, expectations must be kept honest and realistic. Neither wants a campaign that will fail, so this means setting realistic expectations across all aspects. A partner does not want to overpay or over-exchange. It might mean a partner may not meet their ROI, that ultimately leads to a failed partnership. It's not advisable to lie about the number of customers you have, make up unrealistic deadlines, or let the partner down in any way. Remember, you are both in this together.

Example

Exclusive offering from E.ON and Tesco

[73]E.ON is one of Europe's largest electricity providers. They operate in over 30 countries to over 33 million customers. Tesco, at the time of writing, is the largest supermarket in the UK, with stores also across Europe and Asia.

[74]The E.ON and Tesco partnership offers UK customers the exclusive option to exchange Tesco Clubcard vouchers to pay their E.ON energy bills. Here a whole host of campaign elements were agreed, from featuring the offer in the E.ON newsletters, exposure onsite and within direct mail, as well as the agreed communication strategy, tone of voice, use of Tesco branding, and which customers they will target. [75]

The Partnership Agreement

An essential part of the campaign set-up is to agree terms with your partner via a contract. Signing the 'Partnership Agreement' ensures both parties are bound to the campaign and all its elements, as well as acting as a reference point later on. The contract should reference all the campaign assets, agreed commercial terms and copyrights.

All companies should have a legal representative who can write up a contractual agreement, if not there are many templates or examples online. If you do download one, or get sent one by a partner, remember that each contract is individual to the partnership, with specific terms relevant to that campaign. For your use we have included an example of a Partnership Agreement template that should cover many of the general conditions you will need.

There can be times where Partnership Marketing campaigns will run smoothly without a contract in place, but this hugely depends on the situation and level of trust in a partner. This normally happens with very small or short campaigns; one newsletter release, banner placement or short-term sponsorship. Though it is always recommended to have campaign terms in writing somewhere, such as over email.

Partnership Agreement Example

[Campaign Name] Partnership Agreement

This Agreement is dated dd/mm/yyyy

Parties:

[Company Name], a company registered in [Country] with company number X whose registered office is at [Company Address]("Company Name")

And

[Partner Name], [Company Address] ("Partner")

Whereas

[Company Details]

Partner wishes to [purchase/agree to] Advertising Space available on the [Advertising Space Name].

Advertisements are accepted by [Company Name] subject to the following conditions:

The Partner's Promotional Banner must be received by [Company Name] no later than 2 weeks after signing this agreement and the Partner shall supply the Promotional Banner in such format as [Company name] shall specify in writing from time to time.

Acceptance of the Promotional Banner shall not in any way prejudice [Company name] right to reject the Promotional Banner at any time ("Accepted").

[Company name] shall place an Accepted Promotional Banner provided within the Advertising Space as agreed in writing with the Partner from time to time.

[Company name] shall display Accepted Promotional Banner from [Start Date] to [End Date] ("the End Date").

The Promotional Banner shall be displayed and targeted to [Company name] customer base using the [Company name] Mobile Application.

[Company name] shall provide performance tracking information of Accepted Promotional Banner and make results available via the Partner's [Company name] Account.

[Company name] may make any additions to, changes in or deletions from any Promotional Banner required by any competent authority, provided that [Company name] shall inform the Partner prior to making any addition, change or deletion, where reasonably practicable.

It is the responsibility of the Partner to check that the Promotional Banner is correct. [Company name] accepts no liability for any error in the Advertisement, or in the case of multiple Advertisements the repetition of an error unless notified to [Company name] immediately at the point at which the error occurs.

Warranties

The Partner warrants that:

It has the full power and authority to enter into and perform this Agreement;

it complies with all applicable laws, rules and regulations and any industry codes or rules (by which the Partner or [Company name] may be bound) that are in force at the time the Advertisement is to be inserted;

The Advertisement does not contain any material that shall breach any contract or infringe or violate any copyright, trademark or any other personal or proprietary right of any person or render [Company name] liable to any claims or proceedings whatsoever;

In respect of any Advertisement submitted which contains the name or pictorial representation (photographic or otherwise) of any living person and / or any part of any living person and / or copy by which any living person is or can be identified, the Partner has obtained any authority of such living person to make use of such name, representation and / or copy;

The Advertisement submitted is not obscene or libellous;

The Advertisement and any information submitted must be legal, decent, honest and truthful and comply with the British Code of Advertising Practice and all other relevant codes under the general supervision of the Advertising Standards Authority;

Commission

Partner agrees to pay the fees according to the following commission structure: [Insert agreed pricing]

Subject to compliance with this Clause 10, [Company name] reserves the right to render an invoice for the fees as detailed in 10.1. Such invoice shall be rendered on the last day of each month following the commencement of the Term. Partner shall pay the invoice no later than 30 days after the date of issue of the invoice.

[Company name] reserves, at its absolute discretion, the right to remove any Accepted Promotional Banners in the event of non-payment or late-payment by the Partner.

If Partner fails to make any payment due to [Company name] under this agreement by the due date for payment, then, without limiting [Company name]'s remedies under clause 11.

Termination

The initial term of this agreement shall be the period specified under clause 3 above up to the End Date on which date the Agreement shall automatically expire ("the Initial Term").

The duration of the Initial Term may be extended by agreement in writing between the Parties.

Any provision of this agreement that expressly or by implication is intended to come into or continue in force on or after termination or expiry of this agreement shall remain in full force and effect.

Indemnity and Liability

Nothing in these Terms excludes or limits the liability of [Company name] for death or personal injury caused by the negligence of [Company name] or any other liability which may not otherwise be limited or excluded under applicable law.

Subject to clause [Company name]'s aggregate liability (whether in contract, tort or otherwise) for loss or damage shall in any event be limited to a sum equal to the amount paid or payable by the Partner for the Advertising Space in respect of one incident or series of incidents attributable to the same clause.

Subject to clause above, [Company name] shall not be liable in contract, tort (including limitation negligence), pre-contract or other representations (other than fraudulent or negligent misrepresentations) or otherwise out of or in connection with the Terms for any:

Economic losses (including without limitation loss of revenues, data, profits, contracts, business or anticipated savings); or loss of goodwill or reputation; or special or indirect losses suffered or incurred by that party arising out of or in connection with the provision of any matter under these Terms.

The Partner shall indemnify [Company name] against any claim, cost, loss, damage and/or expense that [Company name] may incur as a direct or indirect consequence of [Company name] publishing the Advertisement in accordance with the instructions of the Partner.

Copyright

The Partner hereby grants to [Company name] a worldwide licence to reproduce, display and copy the Advertisement in the [Company name] Mobile Application.

Miscellaneous Provisions

The validity, construction and performance of this Agreement shall be governed by English Law and the parties agree to submit to the exclusive jurisdiction of the English Courts.

[Company name] shall be under no liability for any delay or failure to deliver Advertising Space or otherwise perform any obligation as specified if the same is wholly or partly caused whether directly or indirectly by circumstances beyond its reasonable control.

If any portion of these Terms is held by any competent authority to be invalid or unenforceable in whole or in part, the validity or enforceability of the other sections of these Terms shall not be affected.

No person who is not a party to this Agreement shall have rights under the Contracts (Rights of Third Parties) Act 1999 or otherwise to enforce any term of this Agreement

No delay or failure by [Company name] to exercise any powers, rights or remedies under these Terms will operate as a waiver of them nor will any single or partial exercise of any such powers, rights or remedies preclude any other or further exercise of them. Any waiver to be effective must be in writing and signed by an authorised representative of [Company name].

These Terms including the documents or other sources referred to in these terms and conditions supersede all prior representations undertakings and agreements between the Partner and [Company name] and sets forth the entire agreement and understanding between the Partner and [Company name].

Name, Date & Signed for and on behalf of the [Company Name]

....

Name, Date & Signed by the Partner

…..

The Non-Disclosure Agreement

Aside from contractual agreements some brands also sign an NDA (Non-Disclosure Agreement). This contractually binds both companies to speak freely about their ideas and proposals without the other misusing or copying those plans, or passing them onto a competitor.

Some companies prefer just to sign this and include additional terms so that a contract is not needed. While others prefer to sign this upon initial discussions, then sign the Partnership Agreement once a firm partnership is in place. It is all at the discretion of your legal teams and their stance on this.

Again, there are free templates online, though a legal representative at your company should have a company specific version for you to use. Below is an example to give you an idea of what an NDA consists of.

NDA Example

This Agreement is made on (the "Effective Date") by and between:

(1)   [Company A]
        [Address]

AND

(2)   [Company B]
        [Address]

In connection with a proposed business relationship, the Company has allowed you access, or may allow you access, to business, technical or other information, materials and/or ideas ("Proprietary Information", which term shall include, without limitation, anything you learn or discover as a result of exposure to or analysis of any Proprietary Information).

In consideration of any disclosure and any negotiations concerning the proposed business relationship you agree as follows:

1.   *You will hold in confidence and will not possess or use (except as required to evaluate the proposed business relationship) or disclose any Proprietary Information except in-formation you can document (a) is in the public domain through no fault of yours, (b) was properly known to you, without restriction, prior to disclosure by the Company or (c) was properly disclosed to you by another person without restriction. You will not reverse engineer or attempt to derive the composition or underlying information, structure or ideas of any Proprietary Information. The foregoing does not grant you a license in or to any of the Proprietary Information.*

2.   *If you decide not to proceed with the proposed business relationship or if asked by the Company, you will promptly return all Proprietary Information and all copies, extracts and other objects or items in which Proprietary Information may be contained or embodied.*

3.   *You will promptly notify the Company of any unauthorised release, disclosure or use of Proprietary Information.*

4.   *You understand that this Agreement does not obligate the Company to disclose any in-formation or negotiate or enter into any agreement or relationship. You will strictly abide by any and all instructions and restrictions provided by the Company from time to time with respect to Proprietary Information or the Company systems. You will ensure the security of any facilities, machines, accounts, passwords and methods you use to store any Proprietary Information or to access the Company systems and ensure that no other person has or obtains access thereto.*

5.   *The terms of this Agreement will remain in effect with respect to any particular Proprietary Information until you can document that such Proprietary Information falls into one of the exceptions stated in Paragraph 1 above.*

6.   *You acknowledge and agree that due to the unique nature of the Proprietary Information, any breach of this agreement would cause irreparable harm to the Company for which damages are not an adequate remedy, and that the Company shall therefore be entitled to equitable relief in addition to all other remedies available at law.*

7.   *Until one year after the later of (i) the date of the Agreement or (ii) the last disclosure of Proprietary Information to you, you will not encourage or solicit any employee or consultant of the Company to leave the Company for any reason.*

8.   *This Agreement is personal to you, is non-assignable by you, is governed by the laws of England and Wales and may be modified or waived only in writing signed by both par-ties. If any provision of this Agreement is found to be unenforceable, such provision will be limited or deleted to the minimum extent necessary so that the remaining terms re-main in full force and effect. The prevailing party in any dispute or legal action*

regarding the subject matter of this Agreement shall be entitled to recover solicitors' fees and costs.

Signed for and on behalf of Company A ....

Signed for and on behalf of Company B ....

Following Brand Guidelines

Most brands, due to copyright and trademark law, are extremely protective about their brand. The Partnership Agreement should cover the details on brand terms of use.

There is also another useful document, the Brand Guidelines, that outlines where and how the branding should be used, such as logo design variations, colours and guidelines on tone of voice.

It is a document that most brands have, one that really helps a partner brand understand how to show your branding during the campaign. [76]Below is an example from Skype, outlining the recommended use of their brand logo:

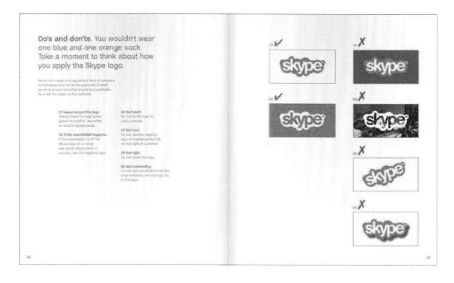

Mutual Terms and Conditions

If the campaign involves any promotional offers, such as an exclusive offer for another brand's customers, then Terms and Conditions will need to be in place.

A Terms and Conditions document is different to the Partnership Agreement as it is customer facing. They should be freely available and accessible for the customer, and provide them with every detail on how they can get the offer.

The legal representative would again be able to assist in the creation of this, if not there are free templates online. Here is an example of the typical terms and conditions page:

T&C's Example

1. This offer is applicable to new customers only. New customers are defined as those who have not previously a customer with Company-X.

2. This offer cannot be used in conjunction with any other new customer promotion or offer. New customers are eligible to collect further Tesco reward points by referring friends to Company-X.

3. In order to validate this offer, the new customer must:

- *Begin the sign-up process on www.company-x.com/tesco and provide a valid Tesco Reward Reward Programme membership number.*
- *Create a Company-x account with the standard minimum opening deposit of £500, as well as committing to £100 monthly contribution, in their account after 23:59 on 25th January 2017 and before 23:59 on 19th February 2017 to collect 5,000 Tesco reward points. Customers who make an initial contribution of £5,000 or more will collect 10,000 points.*
- *Should you wish to open a product-b, there is a minimum investment of £5,000 specifically for this product and you will be awarded 10,000 points.*

4. If a customer withdraws their account balance within 12 months of opening their account, in the event of 5000 points being issued, Company-X reserves the right to withdraw £50 from the closing balance before returning funds. In the event of 10,000 points being issued, Company-X reserves the right to withdraw £100 from the closing balance before returning funds.

5. *Tesco may take up to 45 days to reach your Tesco Rewards account from when we receive an initial contribution to Company-X.*

6. *Only one Tesco reward per new customer.*

7. *Terms and Conditions apply to Tesco redemptions. Reward flights bookings are subject to availability. Tesco points are issued and redeemed in accordance with Tesco terms and conditions may be subject to availability which may be limited or not available. The usual taxes, fees and carrier charges apply to Reward points.*

8. *Nutmeg is the sole arbiter of these rules and any other issue arising under this promotion.*

9. *If gaming of the offer is found, Company-X reserves the right to cancel this promotion and remove any other promotions from the customer's account.*

10. *An invitation to participate in this offer does not provide assurance that you will be accepted as a customer of Company-X.*

11. *Our standard terms relating to your use of Company-X and your account apply and are not affected in any way by this offer.*

12. *This offer is subject to change and Company-X reserves the right to withdraw this offer after 5,000 customers have redeemed, or due to unexpected operational constraints which negatively impact the Company-X customer experience.*

Knowledge Sharing

One overlooked benefit of Partnership Marketing is the opportunity to learn from a partner brand. It is one of the most cost-effective ways of educating staff and gaining insight. Every company is different, each with an assortment of talented personnel, refined processes and industry expertise, all of which can be shared and learnt from. Below are some of the common knowledge sharing themes:

- **Training Sessions** - both sides want the partnership to work, so training sessions can be used to educate and pass on knowledge if a partner lacks skill in a certain area.

- **Product Understanding** - educating one another on the technical details of your product will improve overall understanding. This leads to greater appreciation of the products on sale, which can only benefit the campaign.

- **Past Partnerships Learnings** - explaining the failures of the past partnerships and outlining what improvements were made, will be of great advantage going forward.

- **Marketing Knowledge** - both teams involved should share their marketing knowledge. Teaching each other will only have positive impact on optimisation and conversion.

It is recommended to be open about what you know and what has worked well in the past. Ultimately you want their brand to succeed as much as your own.

Recommended Ways to End a Partnership

Not all partnerships are successful, we must face up to the fact that some partnerships will fail. Therefore, it is useful to know the steps to take to end a failed partnership.

Firstly, a failed campaign doesn't necessarily mean a failed partnership. There may be more than one campaign running with a partner, so if one doesn't succeed it doesn't necessarily mean a partnership must end. In many cases it means learning lessons for the next campaign.

Reasons Why a Partnership Ends

There are multiple reasons why a Partnership may end, some typical reasons are:

- Campaign doesn't achieve objectives
- Disagreement between both parties
- A break of the contractual terms
- Change of management or personnel
- Change in strategic direction
- Closing down of a partner brand

Ways to Manage the Relationship

If the partnership must end, then it is recommended to manage the situation delicately to not burn any bridges. If the campaign has not met its objectives, in most cases it is because of insufficient conversion rates or poor brand engagement. In these situations, it is best to remind a partner that campaign success is never guaranteed and that the best course of action is for each party to review and learn for their future campaigns, therefore keeping the possibility of a future partnership intact.

A breach of contractual terms is a more serious reason for failure. This is why tight contractual terms are put in place to begin with, so in these cases your legal representatives should be involved in finishing the partnerships.

8. Strategy & Planning

Creating an Offer

One of the first strategic decisions is whether you are running a partnership that includes an offer to customers. Most partnerships include some type of offer; however, a partnership can exist without any, such as promoting a partner's new product feature or event.

There are many types of promotional offers, from discounts to prizes:

- Monetary discount
- Percentage discount
- Buy-one get one-free
- Three-for-two
- Additional Prize
- Limited Time Only
- Location Only
- Volume Usage Only

Arranging the Offer

Target Audience:

To create the offer there are several steps to take. Firstly, the brand producing it needs to have a full picture of who they are trying to attract. They should understand their audience in detail, such as the products they use and their average basket size.

Value of Discount:

To decide how much discount to give away in your offer, you need to know your profit margins after offers are applied. If the cost to acquire a new customer is £100, and you acquire them by selling a product for £200 with a 10% discount (selling it for £180), you have made an £80 profit. However, if the customer costs you £200 to acquire then you can't afford to offer any discount.

You can look at discounts on an initial purchase basis such as the above, where there is profit even after a discount is applied, however most business look at it on a long-term basis. This means understanding your customer's Lifetime Value, how much are they worth to you over their full period as your customer, which can often be several years. They look at this because sometimes offering a discount can mean negative profitability on their initial purchase, but in the long-run, after several purchases, it leads to profitability.

Testing:

A brand may have arranged an offer, but will it work and appeal to customers? An offer can be tested on one customer segment before being rolled out to other groups. You could also verify your offer before going live using online forums or focus groups, taking a portion of your target audience and finding out exactly what they think.

Exclusivity:

Exclusivity is where the offer is arranged to be only found through a specific partner's campaign, as oppose to offering a discount across all your marketing channels or across all partners. In my experience customers are far more likely to engage with an offer if it is something they can't get anywhere else, and only through your partner brand. If customers recognise that the offer is exclusive and cannot be obtained anywhere else then the conversion rate is almost always higher than your base rate.

Establishing Brand Positioning

At the Strategy and Planning phase the imagery and positioning of the partnership and the offer is a key consideration; both brands need to agree how it will be displayed, who produces the Creatives, and the message they want to include.

Both partners should have shared Brand Guidelines and negotiated campaign elements. At this stage it is about gathering designs, consulting agencies and pulling together resources.

<u>Creatives & Designs</u>

Creatives should be impactful, attractive and enticing. They should visually promote the uniqueness of the partnership. It should show the relationship between partners, perhaps by including relevant terminology such as 'in partnership with' or by including both logo's. The below image shows how the popular supermarket [77]Iceland agreed for their logo to appear in the Disney's Frozen advert:

<u>Materials</u>

To create the adverts the marketing team should use either in-house designers or an agency. Creative briefs should be written to describe exactly what you are looking for (more on this later in this chapter).

Specific sizes should be prepared based on the partner's requirements. Most brands working online tend to use industry standard banner sizes such as 728x90 – [13]recommended by Google via their AdWords program. My recommendation is to produce an entire range of sizes so that the partner can pick and choose.

Tone of Voice

For Content Partnerships where words play the starring role, the content needs to be in-line with the target audience. If the audience is used to a particular style of writing, then this should be kept to. If the audience is used to particular words or phrases, such as a catchphrase, then these shouldn't differ much either.

Integrated Partnerships

Brands working on Joint Product Partnerships combine their services by integrating with one another. If running these partnerships, the Strategy and Planning phase is important to scope out exactly how this will happen.

What are Integrated Partnerships?

Integrated Partnerships often occur in websites or apps. They are where a primary brand will incorporate the secondary brand's service into their own via white-labelling (a product or service produced by one company rebranded to make it appear as if they had made it) or iframing (an element used to insert content from another source into a web page), often with the use of APIs (is a set of subroutine definitions and data protocols).

The purpose of an Integrated Partnership is to add further value to the customer journey. Instead of a customer having to click away to another app, or open a separate window to get to a partner's app, their services are offered all within one environment. Another benefit is that this allows you to offer another service without having to create it yourself from scratch.

How to plan for it

When it comes to including another brand within your own, you have to start by reaching out to your Product department to understand how adaptable your product is. Do you have the capability to offer your service as a white-label? Do you have an external API you can offer out to third-parties? Or, can your site incorporate an iframe?

If your Product team have confirmed that an integration is possible, then you need to work closely with your, and your partner's, designers, project managers and engineers. Firstly, a designer will need to scope out what the integration will look like on the front-end. Next an engineer will need to determine what needs to be built in the back-end for the idea to come to life. All of this while a project manager determines the timeframes and allocates which engineers will work on each part.

Examples

Starling Bank integrate round-up-investing app Moneybox

[78]In 2017 challenger bank Starling integrated savings app Moneybox. Starling bank aims to offer a mobile first bank account for the digital generation. Moneybox is a savings app that lets you round up each purchase to invest your remaining pennies.

Without a savings product of its own Starling integrated Moneybox so that their users can save seamlessly and invest. It was made possible through iFraming and using open APIs from both companies. This meant data could be transferred between each other so that a customer didn't have to leave the Starling app to create a Moneybox account. The customer journey is easy and seamless.

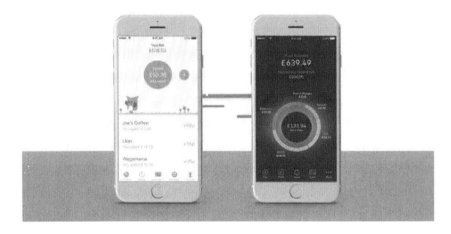

Citymapper lets you request an Uber through their App

[79]Citymapper, the commuter's app, uses opensource data from local transport services to show journey routes, allowing the user to compare various types of transport. Citymapper integrated Uber as a transport option so that you can easily request a taxi for your chosen

journey. The times, prices and ability to request are all done through the Citymapper app. For the user this is quick, easy and convenient.

Tracking

The more data that can be collected, the better understanding a business has on what is going on and what decisions to take. To gather this data, every campaign needs sufficient tracking. At this stage your tracking should be configured so it is all in place before going live with your campaign.

Choose your tracking

As we have two brands marketing under one campaign, it's important to ensure tracking is in place for both companies to measure. Online, we can use cookies and tracking links implemented at different touch points along the user journey. Offline, we can use promotional codes or loyalty cards to track activity. Here are a several tracking options available:

- **PromoID** - added to the end of a URL, and linked to your internal data-warehouse.

- **CouponCodes** - using promotional codes such as 'TicketSale' or '10PercentDiscount'.

- **Third Party Tracking** - affiliate tracking, Adservers, Doubleclick.

- **UTM** - tracked via Google Analytics.

Tools and data

Your decisions here will be specific to your campaign and influenced by the type of partnership you are running, as well as your customer journey's.

Online

What makes online marketing unique is that unlike offline the performance can be proven. Some of the tools mentioned above, such as Google Analytics, affiliate programs, or Doubleclick, are all recommended to track campaigns. Doubleclick is advantageous for programmatic direct-buy campaigns, whereas CAKE is a useful all-round tracking technology. UTM codes, tracked via Google Analytics, are useful too. If you are just starting out in partnerships, they are simple to create and implement, and instructions can be found online.

Offline

Tracking offline is more difficult than online. Every brand that advertises offline experiences the same problem of tracking, with no cookies to track the actions then how do you know exactly the performance of a campaign? Some popular solutions include using CouponCodes, loyalty cards or mobile data. A CouponCode is where a certain code can be taken into a store by a customer, or entered online, allowing the firm to recognise if an offer has been taken up.

In the future companies may use mobile data. Where electronic billboards you walk past will automatically sync with your mobile activity using geolocation, tracking those who search for the advertised brand after they have walked past the ad.

Overall, the industry still doesn't have an effective answer for offline tracking, which is perhaps why so many marketing campaigns are moving online these days.

Ways to Pay a Partner

With paid-for campaigns you must consider how and when payments are made. In the planning phase a decision should be made between both teams. The firm requesting the payment will often dictate the requirements:

<u>Payment Models</u>

- **Revenue Share** - payment is made as a percentage of each referred customer's revenue.

- **CPA** - cost per acquisition; a one-off payment for each customer's initial sale.

- **CPC** - cost per click; paying every time a customer clicks through to your website.

- **CPM** - cost per thousand impressions; paying a partner for every thousand impressions (when an ad is fetched from its source and is countable) their advertisement is shown.

- **Fixed Fee** - a fixed price to the partner.

- **Hybrid** - a combination of any of the above models.

<u>Ways to Pay</u>

- **Invoicing** - partner pays once you have issued them an invoice, this is a statement declaring how much is owed.

- **Automatically** - agreeing to send funds on a set date per period.

<u>When to Pay</u>

- **Advance** - partners agree to payments before or upfront for a campaign.

- **During** - payments made while a campaign is occurring, or on set dates during the campaign; first Monday each week.

- **Arrears** - made at the end of the period, once all results are known.

When it comes to payments there must be an assurance that the partner will pay for the activity, so this should be reflected in the signed Partner Agreement or by using an Insertion Order (a signed document that commitments an advertiser to pay). It should also be agreed who will be tracking the results, to calculate the payments accurately. One, or both, partners can do this, or some choose to use third-party tracking software.

Forecasting, CPA's & ROI

To know how successful a campaign will be, and so whether to go ahead with it, you will need to forecast your results. Potential stakeholders will want to know if the partnership will be worth their time and money.

How to Forecast Campaigns - Example

Company-X have agreed to promote your brand in their popular monthly newsletter, so you will need to decide whether the campaign will be a success. They have offered you a price to pay of £1k for this exposure. You asked Company-X whether they would like to be promoted in your monthly newsletter in return, but they insisted that they would rather the payment than the mutual exposure.

To make this decision you need to ask for two things. Firstly, what are their average open and click through rates for a similar campaign? How many customers will open the Company-X newsletter, and click on your offer? Secondly, what will be the reach? How many Company-X customers will be receiving the newsletter?

Company-X responds with the necessary information. They have informed you the newsletter goes out to 100k customers. The average open rate is 20%, and the clicks to open rate is 10%. You know when a customer comes through an exclusive offer, on average 2% of them make a purchase. That leaves the campaign to look as follows:

Partnership Campaign						
	Target	Open Rate	Clicks	Conversion	Cost	CPA
Newsletter	100,000	20,000	2000	40	£1,000	£ 25.00

The 20% open rates means 20,000 customers are predicted to open the Company-X email, with 10% of those, 2,000 customers, clicking on the link taking them to your website. A 2% conversion rate of these 2,000 customers, means 40 customers will go on to make a purchase with you. The cost per customer (CPA) is worked out by dividing the total cost by the number of newly acquired customers. At a cost of £1k the CPA will therefore be £25, meaning you will be paying £25 for every new customer.

This could be more complex depending on the number of placements. If Company-X offer you several more assets to purchase, all at varying conversion rates, then the forecast could look something like this:

Partnership Campaign Forecast							
	Target	Open Rate	Clicks	Conversion	Cost	CPA	
Monthly Newsletter	100,000	20,000	2000	40	£ 1,000	£	25.00
Weekly Newsletter	50,000	10,000	1500	30	£ 750	£	25.00
Article Feature	6,000	-	600	12	£ 500	£	41.67
Display Ad	75,000	-	750	15	£ 175	£	11.67
	Total			97	£ 2,425	£	25.00

Both newsletters Company-X have offered you have a 20% open rate, but the weekly newsletter has a 15% click to open rate, leading to 70 customers in total, both at a CPA of £25. The article feature is viewed by 6,000 Company-X customers, with a click to open rate of 10% it is forecasted to attract 12 new customers. The display advert is seen by 75,000 customers, but has a much smaller click rate (1%), meaning only a forecast of 15 customers. Therefore, the CPA for the article and ad are £41.67 and £11.67 respectively. Overall the forecasted blended CPA comes to £25; total costs of £2,425 divided by 97 total new customer conversions.

It is important to note that not all campaigns have click through rates. For example, if you are running an offline brand awareness campaign, with no call to action, such as a sponsorship. Here you will need to use the predicted number of people viewing the sponsorship. If you know that 200,000 people will attend an event where your logo will be shown, and based on your industry average 1% of these will view your brand, meaning 2,000 of these will go on to visit your website. You will then need to apply your average conversion rate of 2%, 40 customers, who will go on to make a purchase. This is of course less accurate than click-through figures.

Lastly, brands won't always ask for payment of assets, as Company-X have done here, and as explained in earlier chapters. Many partnership campaigns are also agreed on exchange of assets. To forecast this, the premise is the same as the above, yet in replacement of costs in the table, you can place opportunity costs. Opportunity costs are the value of your assets you are giving away in exchange, which should reasonably equal the price if you purchased the partners assets, or simply the value you internally give to these positions.

ROI

To decide whether the Company-X paid-for campaign is worth running or not, based on your forecast, you need to establish whether the CPA is the right amount or not. Are 97 customers large enough, and is £2,425 too high for your budgets? Will there be a positive return on investment (ROI) in this campaign?

To decide this, you need to know what a newly acquired customer spends on average. If your customers on average spend £60 on their first purchase, and £25 is being spent to acquire each customer, you will be making £35 profit per customer. As you are forecast to bring in 97 customers, the total income will be £5,820 (97 x £60). As your costs are £2,425, your net earnings will be £3,395 (£5,820 - £2,425). Your ROI will be 2.4 (income/cost). If your ROI is over 1, you have achieved a positive return on investment. An ROI of 1 means your income was the same as your costs, you've broken even.

If you have a negative ROI (income/costs is less than 1), you may decide to look at customer's Life Time Value. Their initial purchase may only have been £20, but over the course of their lifetime, your customers spend on average £60. Therefore, if you choose to include total lifetime income, your ROI for this campaign will be positive.

If your ROI is still negative, you would have to go back to Company-X to renegotiate a cheaper price for each placement. Sometimes, even if the ROI is positive, the time and effort it might take to run a campaign may outweigh the monetary returns. In this scenario a judgement call would decide whether it is worth going ahead.

To be more accurate in your forecasting, instead of using your customer's total average spend in your calculations, you could use the average spend for a specific customer segment. For example, if Company-X's targeted customers are mainly men in their 50s, you can use the average spend of your customers in this segment in your calculations instead.

Briefs & Project Road-Map

Once you have completed your forecasts, then both parties should build the campaign materials. The briefs, whether used internally or to give to an agency, are detailed instructions on what campaign materials are needed.

There are many different types of briefs, rarely one agency using the same format as another. Most tend to split them in two; campaign briefs and design briefs. Campaign briefs outline the specifics of a campaign, while design briefs cover the artwork.

<u>Campaign Briefs</u>

A campaign brief is a written document, typically split into four main sections; details, overview, dates, and data. It should be precise and relevant, giving a complete picture of what the campaign entails. It should allow the internal teams of agency to fully understand everything you want them to deliver for you.

- Details - *outlining the campaign name, who owns the campaign, parties involved.*
- Overview - *describing the purpose of the campaign and who it is aimed at, and why*
  - Objectives -*what are the aims of the campaign? KPIs'?*
  - Copy - *what words, tone of voice, tag lines are going to be used?*
  - Images - *what creatives will be used and where will the customer see them?*
  - Call to Actions - *where will the customer click through to your website?*
  - Usability - *what landing pages will be produced?*
  - Tracking - *what tracking method will be used to measure the customer journey?*
  - Testing - *how will all the above be checked and tested?*
  - Responsibilities - *who within the team is responsible for each area?*
- Dates - *what are the delivery dates? Include your project-road map (explained below).*
- Data - *what data will be collected? And what are the key measurements of success?*

- Reporting - *which reports will be delivered and who will prepare them?*
- Segmentation - *which data will be collected from this customer group?*

Design Briefs

Design briefs are mainly used for in-house or agency design teams, so they know exactly what to make for you and how it should look. Designers will want to know the answers to the questions below, these will help them create designs which match your requirements.

- What is the product/service we are promoting?
- Who are we speaking to?
- Why are we speaking to them?
- What do we want them to:
  - Think
  - Feel
  - Do
- How and where are the creatives shown?
- Deliverables – what materials to create?
- Do you have any examples of what you are looking for?
- How will we recognise success?

Your briefs should be as accurate and informative as possible. Most agencies or designers tend to treat a brief as gospel, if it is not on the brief then they won't include it.

Project Road-Map

From the briefs, you and/or your agency should create a detailed timeline of when the campaign specifics and the materials will be delivered. If working with an agency, they should provide you with an entire campaign concept and a finalised road-map. It should look something like the below:

Task	Due Date	NOV																		
		1	2	3	4	5	6	7	8	9	10	11	12	13	14	15	16	17	18	19
Briefs for Design & Copy	4th		█	█	█															
Copy Written	10th					█	█	█	█	█										
Banners Created	10th					█	█	█	█	█										
Banners & Copy QA'd	13th											█	█	█						
Tracking Link Generation	13th													█						
Tracking Link Upload	16th																█			
Banners Upload	18th																	█	█	
Stakeholder Go-live	19th																			█

Creating the Campaign Plan Overview

Now the Strategy and Planning phase is complete, it's recommended to write up what has been organised. In large organisations this is particularly useful for senior stakeholders, as it helps them understand the campaign plans and what's been arranged.

Creating the plan

Using PowerPoint, split into ten main sections, the plan should outline everything from campaign concept to the predicted outcome:

1. **Concept** - the opening section needs to outline the premise of the campaign and who the partner is. What type of partnership is it?

2. **Objectives** - what are the aims of the partnership; acquisition, retention or branding? Which KPIs will be used?

3. **Target** - who will the campaign be targeting? Which customer segments?

4. **Assets** - which media assets are going to be used? And under what commercials?

5. **Exposure** - what agencies are involved? What do the designs look like?

6. **Execution** - who will do what and for when? Include the project road-map as well any other strategic decisions made.

7. **Resources** - who is involved in the campaign? What are their roles in the campaign? Perhaps include snippets of the briefs here.

8. **Risks** - what might go wrong and why? What contingencies are in place? Include contractual agreements and T's & C's here.

9. **Forecasts** - what are the forecasts, CPA's, expected ROI and amount of budget needed? Detail of all workings should be shown.

10. **Expansion** - if the campaign is a success then what additional budget might be needed and how would this be spent?

9. Campaign Launch & Live

Pre-Launch Preparation & Testing

Everything we have discussed so far has prepared us for setting up the campaign, now we move on to pre-launch and pressing the go-live button. One of the main considerations prior to launch is testing.

Materials

The completed creatives need to be put through a series of tests. Once the design teams have finished, both brands need to agree whether they match the briefs and look as planned.

To judge the finished designs, you could pass around internally for stakeholder opinions and feedback. Alternatively, a more scientific approach can be taken, by selecting a very small portion of the target customer base, placing the creatives live for a short period of time, and analysing the conversion and feedback.

Tracking

Ensuring that all tracking links are in the right place and working as they should is vital. To test these, brands can use 'test accounts' to enter the CouponCodes to see if they are working. Other tests can be achieved using Google Analytics, setting a few links live, and analysing the real-time data.

Reporting

If your Analysis team are producing specific reports for this campaign or real-time campaign dashboards, then these need to be briefed in, prepared, and tested prior to launch.

Roadmap & Plans

Both brands need to be confident in the plans they have agreed upon, and have a roadmap in place that has clearly defined deadlines.

Both brands should review this one last time before the campaign goes live, adjusting where necessary.

Example of an expertly executed partnership campaign

The Guardian and Audible Offer Listeners Exclusive Content

[80]Founded in 1821, Guardian News & Media publishes guardian.co.uk now recognised as one of the world's leading news websites, as well as guardiannews.com and the Guardian and Observer newspapers. The newspaper's online edition was the fifth most widely read in the world as of October 2014 and in the UK its combined print and online editions reached nearly 9 million readers.

[81]Audible Inc. is an Amazon company, a leading provider of digital spoken audio information and entertainment on the Internet. Audible's mission is to establish literate listening as a core tool for anyone seeking to be more productive, better informed or more thoughtfully entertained. Audible's content includes more than 100,000 programs from more than 1,800 providers that include leading audiobook publishers, broadcasters, entertainers, magazines and newspaper providers.

The Guardian and Audible partnered together to form The Guardian Audio Edition, an hour-long weekly audio digest produced by the Guardian's award-winning multimedia team. Each audio edition aimed to showcase the very best news, culture and opinion pieces published in the Guardian that week.

The Guardian Audio Edition forms part of a wider partnership between the Guardian and Audible that includes sponsorship of the Guardian books homepage, their weekly podcast and their book review pages. All activity is supported by co-branded advertising across the Guardian, including digital ads on their site and print ads in their main paper.

This is a great example of how a partnership can be expertly run. Everything is pre-tested, all creatives and audio is organised and tested upon launch and then released. And as time has gone on the partnership has expanded with new elements released, further sponsorships occurring, and an expansion of joint products.[82]

Utilising Social Media

After pre-launch testing it's time to press the go-live button. When the button is pressed, both sides should roll out creatives and start promoting the partner to their audience. As the customers start to roll in there are several techniques you can undertake to strengthen campaign performance.

Firstly, social media, which can be used to grow engagement, reach and impact. Compared to a traditional marketing campaign, a partnership campaign means twice the social media reach. From exposure in your own and your partners Facebook, Twitter and LinkedIn pages, as well as their Instagram, YouTube and Snapchat feeds. Below are several methods to get the most out of your social media within a partnership:

Facebook

- Joint Advertising - promoting the campaign within status updates, news feeds, or ads.
- Status Updates - regular updates about the joint campaign via both brands' newsfeeds.
- Page Takeovers - update your profile picture and cover photos to include imagery of the joint campaign.
- Campaign Page - creating a new page for the joint campaign.

Twitter

- Joint Tweets - regular tweets from both parties promoting the campaign to their followers.
- Shared Pictures - saving a collection of shared photos via your Twitter account.
- Page Takeovers - using the page wall for brand takeovers displaying the joint campaign.

LinkedIn

- Joint Content - releasing content highlighting the campaign via the newsfeed.

- Page Linking - linking directly to the partner brand in each other's profile.
- Private Messaging - messaging LinkedIn profiles about the joint campaign.

<u>Example</u>

Innocent promote YesTo through Tweets

[83]Innocent began in 1998 by three entrepreneurs from London who wanted to produce an ethical, all-natural smoothie drink. The company now sells over two million smoothies per week and is 90% owned by The Coca-Cola Company.

Social media is an extremely powerful tool to a brand such as Innocent, especially with such a strong cultural identity and voice. This example shows how they promote their partners, in this case YesTo, an ethical, natural beauty brand, via their Twitter feed. Innocent use social media wisely in all their partnership campaigns, they appreciate its reach and engagement as well as its influence as a channel to boost a campaign.

Utilising Other Departments

Aside from social media, a brand can utilise some of their internal departments to further promote the campaign.

Customer Service

One untapped resource is your customer service team. They speak directly with your customer daily, so who better to promote your campaign? Here are a few ideas you can ask them to try:

- **Promote in conversations** - during or at the end of each call the support team can mention the campaign and the partner offer.

- **Customer Behaviour** - if a customer requests for a specific service on the call, or triggers certain behaviour, perhaps they are an extremely loyal or high-spending customer, then the team could inform the customer of the offer.

- **In-call Ads** - promoting the campaign with spoken adverts while customers are waiting on-hold or in customer service voicemails.

- **Email signatures** - ads at the bottom of all customer service support email signatures.

PR

Along with customer service, the public relations team can have a lot of influence on the reach of a campaign. Some potential ideas for them to promote your campaign are:

- **Publications** - free exposure in newspapers and online publications. This example is from the [84]BBC, who picked up the TripAdvisor and Deliveroo partnership:

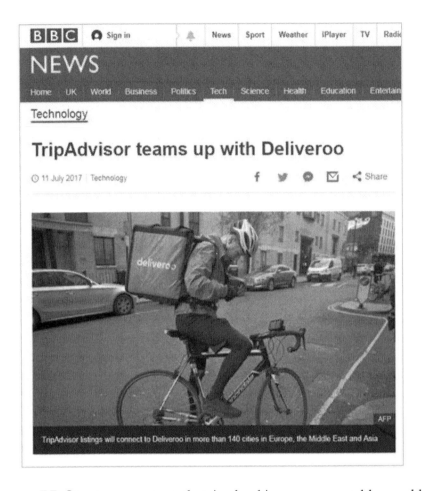

- **PR-Stunt** - any stunt that is shocking or memorable would really help boost exposure, certainly if the stunt goes viral.

Utilising Influencers

Another option to boost performance is to utilise influencers. With the rise of social media, this marketing technique has become extremely popular.

Definition

Influencers encourage others to participate in an event or purchase a product, their decisions and opinions have power to affect their follower's purchasing choices.

Types

Influencers can be placed into three main groups:

1. **Mega-influencers** - actors, artists, athletes and social media stars, for example, who have significant follower base, often 1M+.

2. **Macro-influencers** - executives, bloggers, and journalists who are category specific or industry experts, often with 100,000+ followers.

3. **Micro-influencers** - consumers, budding-celebrities, niche bloggers, who typically have 10,000+ followers.

Influencer Platforms

An influencer actively speaks out on certain topics, and can therefore have huge influence on companies, brands, products and campaigns. They use several different platforms to voice their opinion:

- Blogs
- Social Media
- Word of Mouth
- Social Setting
- Events
- Forums

Finding Influencers

With the rise of social media and digital tools, influencers are becoming easier to find and contact. Here are several ways to locate them:

- **Social** - for certain brands, LinkedIn would be the best tool for finding executives and industry experts. For others, Facebook, Twitter & Instagram would be more effective. All of which show the number of followers and allow you to reach out.

- **Tools** - digital tools help track and monitor influencers, such as Kloud, Traackr and Little Bird. They measure a user's influence across social platforms and assign an influencer score.

- **Agencies** - work with businesses to understand their network and which customers are spreading opinions about their brand.

Managing Influencers

In today's social age, news and gossip spreads fast. For businesses this is both advantageous yet concerning, so they need to be listening to who is spreading both positive and negative opinion, and manage it accordingly. The main methods to manage influencers are:

- **Affiliation** - offering commission to influencers who speak positively about a product and refer customers.

- **Status** - some brands label customers a VIP or Gold member. Show your appreciation to an influencer by offering them a special status.

- **Hospitality** - offer an influencer extra benefits that other customers might not get; hospitality, concierge, or free products.

Both brands should encourage their influencers to positively review the joint campaign. Managed effectively, it will boost campaign performance.

<u>Example</u>

PUMA partner with Argentinian Star

[85]Sergio Aguero is an Argentine professional footballer, playing for English club Manchester City. [86]PUMA is one of the world's leading sport-lifestyle companies that designs and develops footwear, apparel and accessories.

[87]In 2011 PUMA announced its partnership with Sergio Aguero, signing a long-term contract for the Argentine to wear their branded boots. Sergio Aguero has over 11 million Twitter followers and is one of the most active social media influencers in the football industry. As a brand ambassador he encourages a vast wave of his fan base to buy PUMA products by promoting them within his Twitter feed.

In-Campaign Optimisation

Optimisation means making continuous improvements. From your data you should establish where the customers are dropping out of the purchase journey, and make improvements to prevent this. Customers dropping out might be down to various reasons:

- **Varying Offers** - some offers convert better with certain segments. Increasing or improving the discount might prove effective.

- **Varying Creatives** - if the imagery is not enticing enough then perhaps try varying the designs to improve the conversion rate.

- **Messaging** - try altering the content or tone of voice to see if this has any impact.

- **Landing Pages** - try explaining the partnership clearer on the landing page, and improve the CTA's, making them more visible.

- **Terms & Conditions** - maybe the terms of the offer are just too confusing, try making them clearer and easier to find.

- **Click-throughs** - how many clicks does it take a customer to reach the partner's offer? Some say 3 clicks is too many. Try removing some of the steps to conversion.

- **Channels** - if certain marketing channels you're using to promote the partnership aren't proving successful then turn them off and focus on the ones that are. Don't be afraid to move to contingency plans if need be.

Optimisation is about learning and adjusting as you go along to achieve the ideal rate of conversion. Keep testing and improving so your campaign can be as successful as possible.

Managing Multiple Campaigns

Throughout this book we've mainly focused on managing one partnership, though some companies work with many brands across multiple campaigns. Here are two techniques for managing multiple campaigns:

Partnership Timeline

This technique is useful for having an overview on all individual campaigns. Each block within the schedule represents a campaign. Use different colours to relate to different themes. For example, colour green ones to associate to all John Lewis campaigns, red can represent all Debenhams campaigns, while blue all House of Fraser campaigns.

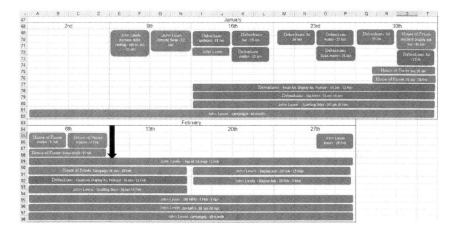

Partnership Funnel

The Partnership Funnel is another method to managing and illustrating multiple partnerships. Here you can categorise partners by what stage they are, from initial contact, all the way to live partnerships.

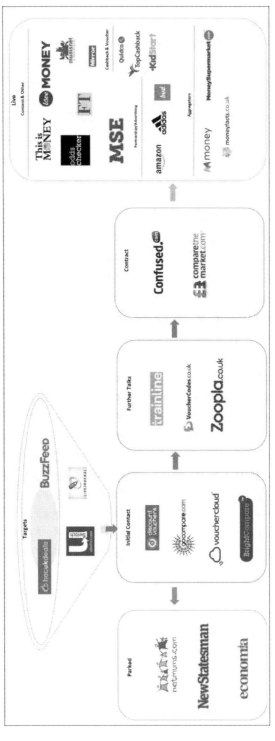

Managing Change

This chapter has been all about in-campaign techniques to influence, optimise and strengthen performance. These can only be achieved on one main condition; the campaign must be adaptable to change. Change is inevitable, nothing goes one hundred percent to plan, so the campaign must have an element of flexibility.

Below are some of the main factors that cause campaigns to change once you're live. These are split between internal and external factors:

Internal

- **Partner Decisions** - a partner may change or alter the stance of a campaign, or there might be a change in personnel, passing the campaign over to a less experienced counterpart mid-campaign.
- **Optimisation** - change doesn't necessarily have to be negative. Like we covered, be prepared to optimise and make changes based on the data to improve results.
- **Promotion** - factors such as social media promotion and utilisation of customer service will also positively influence campaign performance.

External

- **Economic** - alterations in the economic environment, whether globally or in that region, will affect exchange rates, interest rates and inflation that could all have an impact.
- **Competitors** - if a competitor releases a similar campaign or product during the same period it will have a knock-on effect.
- **Stakeholder Influence** - there are many powerful stakeholders (CEO's, CMO's) on both sides who may choose at any time to alter company strategy redirecting the campaign.

It's always important to be prepared for change mid-campaign, whether positive or negative. If negative, refer to your contingency plan you agreed with your partner and make the relevant changes.

10. Results & Analysis

Did the Campaign Achieve its Objective?

Ultimately a partnership campaign will be judged on answering the one main question; did it fulfil its objectives? This book has taken you through, step by step, how to run partnerships and create campaigns. This now leads us onto the final step, the results and analysis.

The performance of a campaign, whether positive or negative, will ultimately be revealed in the data captured throughout the campaign. Both companies now need to analyse the data to answer these questions:

- Did you achieve the original objective?
- Did performance meet the forecasts?
- What was the impact on the target customer group?
- What was the impact on revenue and was there a positive ROI?
- What was the impact upon the brand?

Example

Taking our earlier Company-X example, where Company-X offered their inventory to us, including features in their newsletters, an article feature and display exposure. This is what we originally forecast for the campaign:

Partnership Campaign Forecast							
	Target	Open Rate	Clicks	Conversion	Cost	CPA	
Monthly Newsletter	100,000	20,000	2000	40	£ 1,000	£	25.00
Weekly Newsletter	50,000	10,000	1500	30	£ 750	£	25.00
Article Feature	6,000	-	600	12	£ 500	£	41.67
Display Ad	75,000	-	750	15	£ 175	£	11.67
Total				97	£ 2,425	£	25.00

Let's say we decided to go ahead with this and paid Company-X for the exposure. Our objective was to acquire 97 new customers from the Company-X database, at a cost of £2,425.

We supplied Company-X with our UTM tracking links, and the data was captured through Google Analytics. We now need to analyse whether it met our objective. Whatever tracking method you use (discussed in the Tracking chapter), your data analyst team can also help access the data accordingly.

In our Company-X example, we have gathered the data from Google Analytics and it looks something like this:

Partnership Campaign Results							
	Target	Open Rate	Clicks	Conversion	Cost		CPA
Monthly Newsletter	100,000	21,350	3565	71	£ 1,000	£	14.08
Weekly Newsletter	50,000	8,350	2923	58	£ 750	£	12.93
Article Feature	6,000	-	1068	28	£ 500	£	17.86
Display Ad	75,000	-	218	4	£ 175	£	43.75
Total				161	£ 2,425	£	15.06

If we compare the results above to the original forecasts, we can show the results as follows. Red indicates your results were below forecast, while blue shows a positive result:

Difference - Forecast vs Results							
	Target	Open Rate	Clicks	Conversion	Cost		CPA
Monthly Newsletter	100,000	1,350	1565	31	£ 1,000	-£	10.92
Weekly Newsletter	50,000	-1,650	1423	28	£ 750	-£	12.07
Article Feature	6,000		468	16	£ 500	-£	23.81
Display Ad	75,000		-533	-11	£ 175	£	32.08
Total Difference				64	£ 2,425	-£	9.94

We can also show the difference of the forecasted results against the final results as a percentage, again highlighting negative results in red:

% Difference - Forecast vs Results							
	Target	Open Rate	Clicks	Conversion	Cost		CPA
Monthly Newsletter	100,000	7%	78%	78%	£ 1,000		-44%
Weekly Newsletter	50,000	-17%	95%	93%	£ 750		-48%
Article Feature	6,000		78%	133%	£ 500		-57%
Display Ad	75,000		-71%	-	£ 175		-
Total Difference				66%	£ 2,425		-40%

What the data is showing us, is that the newsletters were far more effective than we predicted. The number of clicks for the monthly newsletter exposure was over 1,565 more than we thought, a 78% increase on forecast. This meant conversions were up by 31, leading to a CPA less than the £25 we predicted, at £14. The weekly newsletter also saw positive results. The open rate was lower than

Company-X told us it could be, but we saw a 35% click through rate rather than 15%, meaning the clicks were 1,423 higher than predicted. The article saw 78% higher clicks than forecast, meaning we converted a total of 28 customers from this at a much lower CPA. Lastly, the display ad, didn't perform as expected, with a lower click rate and conversion than predicted.

In terms of the objective of acquiring new customers, we can certainly say the campaign over-achieved. We acquired a total of 161 customers and all cheaper than we first thought, at £15.06 per customer. Broken down, we have understood that the best value was certainly the weekly newsletter feature, which had the lowest CPA of £12.93.

Analysing Value

Most companies will continue to track customer spend, to see if these customers continue to add value to the campaign. For some campaigns, the costs might not be recouped upon the customers initial spend. It might take several purchases per customer.

In the Company-X example, perhaps the customer's initial average spend was just £10, generating a revenue of just £1,610, against your costs of £2,425, is a loss of £815. However, if you continue to track these customers spend over 2 years, and on average they make 3 more purchases, at £10 each, the revenue from the campaign would be £6,440, a profit of £4,015.

Further analysis can be made if you wish to slice this by segment. Some customer segments will be worth more to you than others, so perhaps 50% will spend £100 over 2 years, worth £8,050, while the other 50% will only spend £20, worth £1,610. This means a combined outcome of £9,660 revenue earned and an ROI of 3.98.

Analysing Other Objectives

This example has focused primarily on acquiring new customers. If your objective was increasing the customer basket size, then the premise is the same, with the comparison on what you spent to promote to them compared to whether they spent more on their purchase.

What is more challenging though, is how to analyse campaigns that focus on brand impact. There are many agencies and tools out there that help gather external data on whether your brand image improved over the time of the campaign. They gather their data by taking pools of people, often via surveys or focus groups, and establish whether your brand is now more recognisable in comparison to how it was before the campaign, and compared to your competitors. Other ways to analyse the impact is to listen to social media. Have your mentions increased, or followers grown? You can also look at your website traffic and sales, did they grow over the campaign period? If so, this indicates that the campaign was a success. Take the figures and compare before and after a campaign period to fully analyse the impact.

Analysing Exchange Campaigns

This section has primarily focused on the Company-X paid-for campaign example, which we covered in the forecast section too. But, what if the campaign was an exchange of assets instead, which many partnership campaigns are. Essentially, the premise when it comes to analysis is the same. Many brands choose to simply replace costs in the tables above, with opportunity costs, or value of assets they give away in return, and therefore the calculations can still run as explained.

It's also important to mention that analysis will not just be contained to your exposure to Company-X's customer base, but also Company-X's exposure to your customer base. This means that their results will also need to be taken into consideration. How well did they convert with your customers? Was their offer enticing? And did it turn out that they acquired the same number of customers at matching LTV to your own? If so, then the campaign can be claimed as a success. With exchange campaigns it's about both sides achieving the objectives they were aiming for, and matching each other's positive ROI.

Summarising the Partnership

The data you have analysed will help determine whether the campaign was a success. But there are other questions to ask, from both sides, to determine if the overall partnership was successful:

- How cooperative was the partner to work with?
- Did they ensure a stable relationship?
- Were full contractual terms met?
- Were payments made and creatives delivered on time?
- Did the partner brand work well with third party agencies?
- Was the partner brand useful in terms of knowledge sharing?
- Did the campaign receive external PR coverage?

At the end of everything, both brands and all stakeholders need to take both the data and the feedback from these questions to decide whether to move forward with any future projects, or now end collaboration.

Partner Scorecard

Some brands like to rate a partner, especially if working with several at a time. Partners can be rated based on answers to certain questions, like the ones above, to determine a score. If the campaign analysis is then placed alongside these answers, it provides a useful picture of an entire partnership.

The Campaign vs The Partnership

There will be instances where a successful campaign can still mean a failed partnership and vice-versa. It is possible for a highly profitable campaign to have been fraught with difficulties. An uncooperative, unresponsive partner can mean a difficult partnership, and one that you may not wish to run again.

On the contrary, a negative campaign with a positive partner means they are the right fit but there might be issues to overcome for future success.

Displaying the Summary

Taking the Campaign Plan Overview document, produced in the planning stage, you can add a section at the end with the final results. Here you can include all your analysis, the answers to the above questions, and the partner scorecard. This then becomes a centralised document on the entire campaign from beginning to end.

Reviewing the Lessons Learned

Partnership Managers on both sides should record all mistakes, to learn from them and prevent future errors. There are several problems that can arise depending on the type of partnership and the campaign:

- **Faulty Tracking** - tracking difficulties normally arise from broken links, faulty promotion codes or poor implementation. This example shows tracked clicks, where a drop off occurred, due to a faulty link:

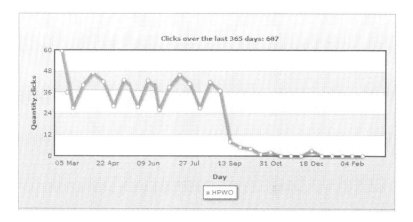

- **Timing Issues** - if either party doesn't follow the agreed timeframes it can lead to delays, over spending, and rushed implementation.

- **Communication Breakdowns** - as we discussed in the Partner Relations chapter, poor communication can lead to problems.

- **Payment Issues** - disagreements when payments are made can cause issues, so ensure that both parties stick to contracted methods.

- **Legal Errors** - a campaign should always follow the exact legal requirements and agreed terms and conditions.

Recording Lessons

Recording all errors and mistakes is vital for future improvements. Both parties should therefore take note of them as they occur throughout the campaign. Google Docs, Asana or SharePoint all allow multiple users in different locations to record mistakes and feedback.

Once they have been recorded a process should be in place to meet up and go through them, to agree how they can be improved upon or eradicated next time.

Long-Term Decisions

Now the campaign has run, the final consideration is to decide whether there will be a longer-term partnership. Would you run the same campaign again but with a different partner, or the same partner but a different campaign? Or perhaps, can you replicate the campaign across multiple partners?

Partnership Marketing isn't a technique to be rushed with huge budgets from the offset. It's about patience, with a test-and-learn approach to find what works best for your customers, and your strategy. In the most part, brands practicing partnerships follow four stages of evolution:

1. **Early Partnership Marketing** - finding your feet with partnerships, testing campaigns, and working with one or two brands. This involves smaller budgets and a lot of exploration.

2. **Multiple Campaign Stage** - once several campaigns have been run, many Partnership Marketing departments decide to expand on their winning formula with multiple brands, working with larger budgets across a variety of campaigns.

3. **Expansion Stage** – next, most departments increase their spending even further, and turn their efforts to targeting segmented multi-partner campaigns. They move from lesser known brands into more mainstream, and create partner pages and large-scale integrations.

4. **Partnership Program** - when brands are experienced in partnerships they create a dedicated Partnership Program, to automate as much as possible. Partners can then sign up, view campaign schedules and book a partnership, take assets and promote your brand at any time.

Partnership Marketing doesn't have to be small with one or two partners, it can be as large and as automated as you can handle. Most companies focusing their efforts on stages 1 and 2 are both cautious yet specific in their approach. While stages 3 and 4 are certainly possible for many, depending on their appetite and budgets. Long-term, Partnership Marketing can be the very factor that influences the fortunes of your business.

Ten Main Takeaways

The principal aim of this book was to introduce, to the digital marketing generation, the potential of Partnership Marketing. Hopefully the step-by-step format has now meant you understand how to run a partnership campaign from beginning to end, and you can pick this up at any time as guide to help you along the way. As a summary there are 10 main points about Partnership Marketing:

1. It is not a marketing channel, but a marketing technique that can be interwoven within every channel.

2. It has 10 distinct types.

3. It can help you achieve all your traditional marketing objectives.

4. Your media assets are the heart of your partnership. They can be paid-for or exchanged.

5. The right partner is one that resonates with your customer base.

6. Make sure all terms and contracts are in-place once you have agreed to work together.

7. Track, forecast, and create a project plan to ensure the campaign runs as smooth as possible.

8. Test, optimise, and utilise other departments to get the best out of your joint campaign.

9. Analyse and review your lessons learned to ensure a long-term partnership.

10. Follow the four stages of Partnership Marketing evolution so that your business is the most advanced it can be.

GLOSSARY

Acquisition - one of the core marketing objectives and literally means attaining a new customer. Also see 'Cost per Acquisition'.

A-B Test - is a method of testing effectiveness. It determines which single variable is the most effective in improving conversion rates to a campaign.

Account Management - a department within the organisation that deals with the day-to-day management of customer accounts. An account manager is a point of contact, and provides customer support, upselling, technical assistance and relationship management.

Added-value - increasing the worth and power of an asset. A high number of consumers or strong brand image helps add value to an asset. A brand can charge more for the asset if it has more customers.

Add-ons - relates to product extensions, where an extra gift, compartment or related product is included within the original offering.

Ad-exchange - a technology platform that facilitates the buying and selling of media advertising inventory from multiple ad networks. Prices for the inventory are determined through bidding.

Ad-space - is the section of a website that is allocated for advertising.

Ad-spot - see 'Ad-space'.

Advertiser - is the website owner or merchant who pays affiliates for sending traffic to their site to purchase or generate leads.

AdWords Program - Google AdWords is their online advertising program that is used for PPC campaigns and allows you to choose where your ad appears, set a budget and measure the conversions.

Affiliate Program - is a marketing program where the affiliate can access to gather marketing materials to promote a merchant brand, and track and record their sales.

Agency - a service dedicated to creating, planning, and handling design or marketing tasks for its clients.

Ambassador - or Brand Ambassador is a person who is hired an organisation or company to represent a brand in a positive light and by doing so they help to increase brand awareness and sales.

ARPU - abbreviation of average revenue per user or sometimes known as average revenue per unit, it is measured by dividing the total revenue by the number of customers.

Asset Audit - is an overview of the areas that a primary brand can offer a secondary brand for exposure. The audit is therefore a complete record of all these possible assets.

Asset Calendar - is used for those running multiple campaigns with many partners and is a list of those assets used under agreed dates per campaign.

Asset Placements - with reference to the Asset Calendar describes the number of positions available for an asset to appear.

Asset Portfolio - is a graphic representation of the Asset Audit, often in the form of a PowerPoint deck. This document is used to show a partner what assets you as a brand have on offer.

Audience Figures – references the number of people of watched a television programme. Although also relates to the number of people who viewed a particular advert or attended an event.

Awareness - is the extent to which a brand is recognised by customers and is correctly associated with their particular product or service. Quantitatively it can be expressed as a percentage of the target market.

B2B - abbreviation of business-to-business, is the exchange of products, services or information between businesses, rather than between businesses to consumers.

Basket Size - aside from the economic terminology of Basket Size meaning the fixed selection of items which is used to track inflation, from a marketing perspective it relates to the average spend of a customer.

BI - abbreviation of business-intelligence. A department found in most business that along with CRM teams have overview of customer data. They can provide spreadsheets, reports and insights into requested data queries.

Bounce Rate - the percentage of visitors to a particular website who navigate away from the site after viewing only one page.

Brand Culture - are the values, decisions, and atmosphere that the company lives and breathes. It is the internal and external perception that pulls through to the customer experience and product offerings.

Brand Ethics - refers to the moral principles and standpoint of particular marketing issues that are matters of moral judgment.

Brand Guidelines - shows where and how the brand should be used, including logo design variations, colours, and tone of voice. They ensure the brand is safeguarded and used correctly.

Brand Image - the general impression of a product, service and company that constitutes as a brand that is held by existing or potential consumers.

Brand Recognition - the extent to which a consumer can correctly identify a particular product or service just by viewing the product or service's logo, tag line, packaging or advertising campaign.

Briefing - providing the information required for a campaign or for the creation of materials in the form of a written document describing what is required, the 'brief'.

Budget - not to be confused with a forecast, refers to the amount of funds one has to spend. A Marketing Budget is the amount a team can spend over a given period/campaign.

Campaign Assets - any area that a primary brand can utilise to provide exposure to a secondary. It refers to any space given to a partner brand that will provide them with the relevant exposure to the customer base.

Campaign Road Map - also referred to as a Project Roadmap, is a high-level outline of the key campaign components showing what tasks are required. It is a step by step list of actions that need to be undertaken by each party.

Category Leader - a stand out brand with regards to recognisability is referred to as 'category leader', with the 5 key components; Age & History, Reputation and Credibility, Market Share, Logo & Culture, Popularity.

Clicks - refers to the number of times visitors have taken the action or facility to press onto a hyperlink to another file or web page.

Click-through - the proportion of visitors to a web page who follow a hypertext link to a particular site. Also used within the context of 'click-through rate' which refers to the percentage or ratio of visitors who took the action.

Co-branded - a product or service marketed under or carrying two or more brand names. Co-branded designs contain two or more brand logos and imagery.

Cohort – similar to a segment or segmentation, it describes a group of customers with similar attributes, whether that be age, location or spend.

Commercials - the agreed price for a particular negotiation. In Partnership Marketing it refers to what a brand is selling or exchanging their assets for; what are the costs to the secondary brand and what both have agreed to.

Commission - a sum, typically a set percentage of the value involved, paid for a commercial transaction.

Competitive Analysis - analysing your competition, their market share, selling points and attributes to establish what makes your product or service attract your target market.

Competitive Bidding - during partnership negotiations there can be a case of 'competitive bidding' where partners are played off against one another to increase the price of your marketing assets.

Conversion Rate - the percentage or ratio of visitors who take a desired action. For example the percentage of customers who click on a CTA.

Copy - simply means text, predominantly used in design briefs. A CTA will often have given text like 'Click here', this can also be referred to as the copy. 'Body Copy' referring to the main text of the content.

CPA - abbreviation of Cost per Acquisition. It is the cost or price of attaining a new customer.

Creatives – also referred to as 'materials' relates to the items created by design teams for use in a marketing campaign; the visual banners and imagery used in a marketing asset.

CRM - abbreviation of Customer relationship management, refers to practices, strategies and technologies that companies use to manage and analyse interactions and data throughout the customer lifecycle, with the goal of improving customer relations.

CTA - abbreviation of Call to Action, is an instruction to the audience to provoke a response, usually using an imperative verb such as "call now", "find out more" or "visit today".

Customer Groups - see 'Customer Segments'.

Customer Journey - describes the series of interactions or steps customers take with a company via all its available channels. It refers to their entrance point all the way to exit areas via CTA's and webpages.

Customer Lifetime Value - shows how much a customer is worth across their entire Customer Lifecycle. The Lifecycle is their period of time spent as a customer with the brand. Not to be confused with CPA which refers to the cost associated in recruiting them as a customer.

Customer Profile - a descriptive profile for each of your customer segment types. It outlines their key characteristics such as Age, Location, Lifestyle and Habits. It helps answer the question, who are your customers?

Customer Proposition - proposition literally means proposal, as in what a brand is offering. The customer proposition therefore describes what is being offered to the customer and why they should buy it.

Customer Segments - are customer groups that share similar characteristics. These characteristics relate to the Customer Profiles, with those who are closely linked grouped together. This can be based on their Age or Income, the cost to acquire them, or their customer journey. Names for such groups include VIP, Non-VIP, new customer, repeat, product preference.

Deliverables - something that has to be provided, especially as a product of a development process, or for creative teams and agencies to deliver back on time.

Department Work Log - an overview of a department's work activity. Often in the form of a report or a calendar, through use of such tools as Confluence, it aids resource management.

Differentiate - to set apart or aside, to stand out. To make or become different in the process of growth or development.

Display - also referred to as 'display advertising' is a type of online advertising that unlike text-based ads, relies on images, audio and video to communicate a message.

Dormant - also referred to as an 'inactive customer' is one who has shopped with you in the past, but has gone an extended amount of time without making another purchase.

Drop-off Rates - the percentage of customers that did not complete a particular action. Essentially dropping out of the sales-cycle, the customer journey, did not fully engage in the campaign, or left the website or shop.

EBITDA - a figure that equates to the true profit figures; earnings before Interest, Taxes, Depreciation and Amortization.

Email Blast - sending multiple electronic messages to many people at the same time. Also used to reference the terminology of Newsletters or Emails being sent to multiple people.

Endorsement - the act of saying that you approve of or support something or someone. Often refers to a famous person supporting a product.

Engagement - is any action a consumer takes with your brand. It is the interaction between the consumer and the product or service activities.

Entrances - an act or instance of entering a website, a store, campaign or Customer Journey and Lifecycle.

Exchange Campaign - where both partners agree to promote each other's services in return for exposure on the opposing partner's side.

Exclusivity - is defined as a state of being limited or hard to access. It is where one brand provides a specially arranged offer for another brand's customer base that can only be found through that partner.

Execution - the carrying out of a plan, order, or course of action. Completion of the steps required to carry out a campaign.

Exit Page - is the last page accessed during a visit; the last page visited on a website or navigation journey.

Exposure - degree to which an audience, readers, listeners, viewers, visitors to a website, is in receipt of a promotional message.

FAQ - a list of questions and answers relating to a particular subject, especially one giving basic information for users of a website.

Focus Group - a group of people assembled to participate in a discussion about a product before it is launched, or to provide feedback after a campaign or event.

Forecast - the calculation or estimate of future events, particularly the effectiveness of a campaign and predicted trends.

GA - abbreviation of Google Analytics is a free web analytics service offered by Google that tracks and reports website traffic.

Go-live - shortened way of saying 'going live'. A product, computer system, campaign, event or project beginning or becoming operational.

Google Docs - is a free web-based application in which documents and spreadsheets can be created, edited and stored online. Files can be accessed from any computer with an Internet connection.

Go-to Market - also referred to as go-to-market strategy is an action plan that specifies how a company will reach customers and achieve competitive advantage. It is a blueprint for delivering a product or service to the end customer.

Historical Data - past-period data, data taken over a period of time. Used usually as a basis for forecasting the future data or trends.

Hospitality - relating to or denoting the business of entertaining clients, conference delegates, or other official visitors.

Hybrid - something made by combining two different elements. A Hybrid deal is one that combines different payment models, such as Revenue Share and a fixed amount.

iFraming - is an HTML document embedded inside another HTML document on a website.

Impression - an instance of a pop-up or other web advertisement being seen on an Internet user's monitor.

Influencers - those that encourage others to participate in an event or purchase a product, their opinions have direct power to affect their followers' purchasing choices.

Infographic - a visual representation of information or data, e.g. as a chart or diagram.

Keyword - a word used in an information retrieval system or search engine such Google to indicate the content of a document or a significant stand out word mentioned in the text.

KPI - abbreviation of Key Performance Indicator's, are measurements of an objective. A KPI is often a number that provides a quantifiable meaning to the results. It therefore describes whether the objective was met or not.

Leads - otherwise known as 'lead generation' is the initiation of consumer interest or inquiry into products or services of a business. Also called a prospect is one that is yet a registered customer who has made a purchase, rather a potential customer.

Lifecycle - otherwise referred to as the 'product lifecycle' describes the stages a product goes through from when it was first conceived until it is finally removed from the market. A 'customer lifecycle' refers to their customer lifetime from lead to dormant customer.

Lifetime Value - see 'Customer Lifetime Value'.

Links - is a hyperlink between web pages or text in documents. Once clicked on a link will take you to a new webpage.

Loyalty Programme - a rewards program offered by a company to customers who frequently make purchases. A loyalty program may give a customer advanced access to new products, special sales coupons or free merchandise.

Loyalty Store - is where rewards from the Loyalty Programme can be purchased. Rewards include physical gifts, cash, or partner offers. These rewards can only be bought by using earned Loyalty Points.

Marketing Asset - is any area that a primary brand can utilise to provide exposure to a secondary one. It literally refers to any space provided to a partner brand that will provide them with the relevant exposure to the customer base.

Marketing Channel - not to be confused with a Marketing Asset, is a type of marketing to be used to create awareness. This can be for example Social Media, Email or through PR. Also referred to as Marketing Avenue, it describes which route will be taken.

Mass Appeal - appealing as a brand or product to the entire market rather than individual market segments or niche customer groups.

Materials - similar to Deliverables and Creatives, describes the elements that need to be produced for each asset. Examples such as banners, a piece of content, a finished advert, a white-paper.

Media Value - providing a numeric value to media coverage such as a TV advert or a newspaper advert. There are often industry values depending on the media and the amount of coverage achieved.

Mind-Map - is a graphical way to represent ideas and concepts. It is a visual thinking tool that helps structuring information.

Minisite - is a website that offers information about one specific product or product group. Typically a minisite is a shorter enhanced multimedia site used for promotional campaign activity, it can also be used to present a range of advertising spaces or a loyalty store.

NDA - abbreviation of non-disclosure agreement. A legally enforceable contract that creates a confidential relationship between a person who holds some kind of trade secret and a person to whom the secret will be disclosed.

Niche - a specialized, particular or specific topic, subject or category. In marketing it refers to the Unique Selling Point and what makes a brand stand out; what is a brand or product's specific quality.

Non-VIP - is a type of Customer Segment that often refers to a customer that isn't considered of VIP status, meaning they are not considered the high spenders more-so the general user and average spender.

One Pager - a term for a document of no more than one page. It is often a consolidated version of a much larger document only displaying the high-level information.

One-off buyer - a customer that only makes one purchase, then doesn't return or continue purchasing.

On-site - referring to activity taking place on a website, also known as Online. As oppose to Off-site or Offline which refers to activity in the physical world.

Opportunity Cost - the loss of other alternatives when one alternative is chosen.

Optimisation - the process of modification to your site and ads to improve the quality, traffic and performance. Based on your goals, optimisation can achieve the optimal, greatest possible, results.

Page Takeover - sharing your social pages or other website real estate with another in terms of imagery used, joint branding and joint updates.

Paid-for Campaign - where the primary brand offers out their marketing assets to a secondary brand but does not request an exchange of exposure in return, instead they sell the assets at an agreed price.

Past Campaign Analysis - accessing the effectiveness of past campaigns, and using this information to benefit the planned Partnership campaign.

Permissions - state officially who is allowed to create, open, have access to or act on a particular project and provide consent or authorisation.

Personalisation - tries to make a unique product offering, promotional offer or serviced approach for each customer. It uses exact data targeting to relate the offering to the individual.

Pivot Tables - allows you to extract the significance from a detailed data set and display this in the form of a table. It will allow you to manipulate the date and comparing accordingly.

Point-of-sale - the place at which a transaction is carried out. Often associated to a retail cashier.

PPC - also called cost per click, is an internet advertising model used to direct traffic to websites, in which advertisers pay the publisher when an ad is clicked. It is defined simply as "the amount spent to get an advertisement clicked."

Primary Brand - refers to the first brand in context as oppose to the secondary brand. The primary is the lead brand, the first to open discussions or initiate the Partnership, the one running the Paid-for Campaign or the one operating the majority of the campaign.

PRINCE2 - abbreviation of 'PRojects IN Controlled Environments', is a process-based method for effective project management.

Procurement - the action of obtaining or procuring something. Referred to as the internal department that works with supplier selections, on receipts and payments, contracts and inventories.

Product Developers - the personnel or department involved in developing, creating and constructing a new product.

Product Perception - how consumers think and understand your product. The perception is what the product means to them. Closely linked to Branding and Culture but focused more on the use of the product rather than the name behind it.

Project Management - is the discipline of initiating, planning, executing, controlling, and closing the work of a team to achieve specific goals and meet specific success criteria.

Promotional Stand - also known as a Display Stand is a dedicated area to a brand's product that highlights its offerings, occasionally manned by the brand's personnel and giving away testers, trials or discounts.

Proofing - the act of proof reading, meaning to read, mark and correct any errors in a written document.

Prospecting - the act of seeking potential new customers. A prospect is a hopeful or a possible customer, and essentially means seeking Leads.

Publisher - those that are willing to promote and advertise a primary brand by advertising/publishing it on their websites.

Pulling Power - will customers be drawn to the brand and their offer? It is the amount of attraction that a brand has to ultimately engage and convert.

Reactivation - is the process of encouraging dormant customers, those that have made a purchase in the past, to purchase once again.

Recognisability - see 'Brand Recognition'.

Re-engage - see 'Engagement'.

Registrations - see 'Sign up's'. Refers to those that have completed a registration form and haven't necessarily made a purchase yet.

Repeat Visit - is one who returns back to a website or store on multiple occasions. Their Repeat Visit is where they have returned for a second, third or more times.

Re-purchase - is a Repeat Visitor who makes another purchase upon that second visit. A Re-purchaser is one who is becoming a loyal customer and who has therefore been retained through the customer lifecycle.

Reputable Brand - a brand that has specific appeal to customers, with engaging offers and be willing to participate in an innovative partnership, one that customers know and understand instantly.

Resonates - means engagement, interaction, where customers understand what the brand or offer relates to. Resonation means to connect with.

Retention Rates - the frequency in which a customer returns to make a purchase. Improving this means encouraging users to return more often, increasing the rate.

Road-map - a plan or strategy intended to achieve a particular goal. The plan outlines what will be created, who will create it, and when for.

ROI - abbreviation of Return on Investment. Is the benefit to the investor resulting from an investment compared to the costs involved. A high ROI means the investment gains compare favourably to the investment cost.

Seasonal Promotion - a promotion occurring around specific times of the year such as Christmas. Seasonal often means that they happen every year or can be foreseen scheduled in a calendar, such as a promotion for the Olympics.

Secondary Brand - refers to the second brand in context as oppose to the primary brand. The secondary is the one approaching the primary for collaboration, the one paying for exposure, the brand following the primary's lead or the 'partner' in reference to the primary brand running the campaign.

Segments - see 'Customer Segments'.

SEO - abbreviation of Search Engine Optimization. Is the process of affecting the visibility of a website or a web page in a search engine's unpaid results, often referred to as natural, organic, or earned results.

Sharepoint - is a browser-based collaboration and document management platform from Microsoft. It allows groups to set up a centralized password protected space for document sharing.

Sign up's - means new customers. A Sign Up is used for brands whose customers must register to use their service. Skype or Spotify are good examples of this.

Site Takeover - see 'Page Takeover', although can reference more an entire website or minisite takeover, rather than one website page or social page.

Smart Marketer - in the same way that SMART objectives are; Specific, Measurable, Achievable, Relevant, Timely, so a Marketer can be thoughtful in their method; a clever Marketer that considers all options and takes a scientific data driven approach.

Social Feed - a list of your social activity with frequently updated content including videos, images and text. Commonly found on Social Media's such as Facebook and Twitter.

Spend Frequency - how often a consumer or customer segment make a purchase.

Stakeholders - any person with an interest or concern in something, in this case an interest in the Partnership and its success.

Standard Offer - what a brand normally offers their customers in terms of a promotional discount or offer, and can be found in the majority of stores. It is opposed to an Exclusive Offer that is specific to a partner brand or customer segment.

Super VIP - is a type of Customer Segment that refers to a very high spending customer. As a Super-VIP they are considered in your top percentile of important customers.

Target Audience - the intended audience or readership of an advertisement or promotional message. They are the specific customer segment you as a brand are aiming the advertising and promotion towards.

Targets - are the Forecast that are set as an objective to achieve. A target is an aim, therefore targets are those set for a particular campaign to achieve.

Test Accounts - a test customer or practice account. These are not real users, rather allow Marketers to test and practice scenarios.

Thought-Leadership - are the informed opinion leaders and the go-to people in their field of expertise. Working on Thought-Leadership is taking on tasks, such as producing White Papers, to portray your company as an opinion leader.

Tone of Voice - it is not what a brand says but how they say it. It's their language, the way it is constructed and brand's personality in their communications.

Usability - is the ease of use, intuitiveness and learnability of a designed object, application or website.

USP - abbreviation of Unique Selling Proposition. Is a factor that differentiates a product from its competitors. Thought of as, what you have that competitors don't.

Value Proposition - an innovation, service, or feature intended to make a company or product attractive to customers. What the brand is offering with their product, it is closely linked to the USP, the stand out feature.

VIP - is a type of Customer Segment that refers to a high spending customer or the very important customer due to their loyalty.

Visibility - similar to Awareness and Recognition, describes how clear, available and easy to find the brand, product or promotion is. Higher Visibility means the more likelihood of customers seeing your campaign.

Webpage - a hypertext document connected to the World Wide Web. Essentially a page of a website.

White Paper - is an authoritative report or guide that informs readers about a complex issue and presents the issuing body's thoughts on the matter. It is meant to help readers understand an issue, solve a problem, or make a decision.

Word of Mouth - oral or written recommendation by a satisfied customer to the prospective customers of a good or service.

NOTES

NOTES

REFERENCES

All text indexed in this reference section highlights the source of information where this has been obtained. All brands mentioned are purely for contextual, informative use, and not to promote any one brand over another or for affiliation purposes of the author.

These references are to indicate that all information in this book has been created by the author aside from the indexed below, of which names of real brands and real, actual examples, as well as images have been taken from public sources to help illustrate the point, and assist with the teachings of this book.

1. What is Partnership Marketing: Amazon run affiliation programmes (https://affiliate-program.amazon.co.uk/)

2. What is Partnership Marketing: FC Barcelona featuring UNICEF (http://foundation.fcbarcelona.com)

3. What is Partnership Marketing: Nexus phone powered by Google (https://en.wikipedia.org/wiki/Google_Nexus)

4. What is Partnership Marketing: Virgin Media is the first provider (http://store.virginmedia.com/digital-tv/channels/netflix.html)

5. What is Partnership Marketing: Netflix is the world's largest on-demand (https://en.wikipedia.org/wiki/Netflix)

6. What is Partnership Marketing: Their partnership formulated in 2013 (http://www.telegraph.co.uk/technology/news/10298644/Netflix-added-to-Virgin-Media-UK-pay-TV.html)

7. Difference between Business and Marketing Partnerships: Pruhealth (https://en.wikipedia.org/wiki/VitalityHealth)

8. Difference between Business and Marketing Partnerships: Virgin Active is considered (http://www.virginactive.com/)

9. Difference between Business and Marketing Partnerships: Pruhealth offer their customers 50% off Virgin Active
(http://www.pruhealth.co.uk/vitality/partners/virgin-active/)

10. Difference between Business and Marketing Partnerships: Pruhealth and Virgin Active Image
(http://www.pruhealth.co.uk/)

11. Affiliation: CAKE
(http://getcake.com/)

12. Affiliation: Income Access
(http://incomeaccess.com/)

13. Affiliation: Linkshare
(http://marketing.rakuten.com/affiliate-marketing)

14. Affiliation: Commission Junction
(http://www.uk.cj.com/)

15. Affiliation: Affiliate Window
(http://www.affiliatewindow.com/uk/)

16. Affiliation: Groupon
(https://www.groupon.co.uk/)

17. Affiliation: Quidco
(http://www.quidco.com/)

18. Affiliation: Moneysupermarket
(http://www.moneysupermarket.com/)

19. Affiliation: Confused
(http://www.confused.com/)

20. Affiliation: The Daily Mail
(http://www.dailymail.co.uk/)

21. Affiliation: TopCashback

(https://www.topcashback.co.uk/)

22. Affiliation: Gocompare
(http://www.gocompare.com/)

23. Affiliation: LG for example, the popular TV manufacture
(http://www.lg.com/uk)

24. Affiliation: Money.co.uk
(https://www.money.co.uk/savings-accounts/investment-isas.htm)

25. Affiliation: IG
(https://www.money.co.uk/savings-accounts/investment-isas.htm)

26. Affiliation: Money.co.uk image
(https://www.money.co.uk/savings-accounts/investment-isas.htm)

27. Content: The web is content and search engines, such as Google
(https://www.google.co.uk/)

28. Content: YouTube
(https://www.youtube.co.uk/)

29. Content: Lonely Planet and British Airways Partnership including the image
(http://www.exterionmedia.com/uk/who-we-are/our-blog/lonely-planet-and-ba/)

30. Content: Lonely Planet Ultimate Experiences image, screenshot of
(http://www.exterionmedia.com/uk/who-we-are/our-blog/lonely-planet-and-ba/)

31. Distribution: Domino's & Virgin Wines
(https://www.marketingweek.com/2009/01/01/dominos-partners-with-virgin-wines/

32. Charitable: Corporate Partnerships
(http://www.institute-of-fundraising.org.uk/code-of-fundraising-practice/sections/corporate-partnerships/)

33. Charitable: Innocent Smoothies
(http://www.innocentdrinks.co.uk/)

34. Charitable: Comic Relief
(https://www.rednoseday.com/partners/sainsburys)

35. Charitable: Sainsbury's
(https://livewellforless.sainsburys.co.uk/about-red-nose-day-2015/)

36. Charitable: Sainsbury's image from
(http://www.allthingsic.com/wp-content/uploads/2013/03/Screen-Shot-2013-03-11-at-21.20.51.png)

37. Joint-Products: LG create Prada branded phone
(http://www.lg.com/uk/press-release/prada-and-lg-create-a-statement-in-style)

38. Joint-Products: Nike and Apple
(https://www.apple.com/uk/pr/library/2006/05/23Nike-and-Apple-Team-Up-to-Launch-Nike-iPod.html)

39. Joint-Products: Nike and Apple image from
(http://assets.ilounge.com/images/uploads/nike-kit-box-2.jpg)

40. Licencing: Angry Birds and Star Wars
(http://www.forbes.com/pictures/femj45gij/angry-birds-partnership-with-star-wars/) (http://www.starwars.com/games-apps/angry-birds-star-wars)

41. Loyalty: British Airways and American Express
(https://www.americanexpress.com/uk/content/ba-credit-card/)

42. Loyalty: British Airways and American Express image from
(https://www.americanexpress.com/uk/content/ba-credit-card/)

43. Product Placement: Yes Man and Ducati
(http://www.motorcycle-usa.com/2008/12/article/ducati-hypermotard-featured-in-film-yes-man/)

44. Shared-Stores: Cineworld & Starbucks
(https://en.wikipedia.org/wiki/Cineworld)

45. *Shared-Stores: Cineworld & Starbucks image from*
(http://www.cineworld.co.uk)

46. *Sponsorship: The English Football Premier League*
(https//en.wikipedia.org/wiki/Premier_League)

47. *Sponsorship: Barclays*
(https://www.home.barclays/)

48. *What are the Partnership Objectives & KPIs?: Etihad Airways &*
Manchester City
(http://www.etihad.com/en-us/about-us/our-sponsorships/football/mcfc/)

49. *Examples of Campaign Objectives: Starbucks and New Look*
(http://www.starbucks.com/store/2407/gb/london-colney-new-look/colney-fields-shpg-ctre-barnet-rd-london-colney)

50. *Examples of Campaign Objectives: Summer Series Music Festival partners*
with American Express
(https://www.somersethouse.org.uk/music/summer-series-2015)

51. *Examples of Campaign Objectives: PayPal is an American company*
(https://en.wikipedia.org/wiki/PayPal)

52. *Examples of Campaign Objectives: PayPal screenshot from*
(https://www.paypal.com/deals/offers)

53. *What are Partnership Marketing Assets?: Secret Escapes*
(http://mp.secretescapes.com/hunter/)

54. *What are Partnership Marketing Assets?: Hunters Boots*
(http://mp.secretescapes.com/hunter/)

55. *Examples of Utilising your Online Assets: Barclaycard*
(https://www.barclays.co.uk/uber-offer/)

56. *Examples of Utilising your Online Assets: Uber*
(https://www.barclays.co.uk/uber-offer/)

57. Examples of Utilising your Online Assets: EasyJet is a British airline (https://en.wikipedia.org/wiki/EasyJet)

58. Examples of Utilising your Online Assets: Founded in 1996 Booking.com (http://www.booking.com/content/about.en-gb.html)

59. Examples of Utilising your Online Assets: In 2012 both brands (http://www.travpr.com/pr-13926-easyjet-and-bookingcom-strike-new-hotel-agreement.html)

60. Examples of Utilising your Online Assets: EasyJet also collaborate with Europcar (http://corporate.easyjet.com/latest-news-archive/news-year-2003/01-07-03-en.aspx?sc_lang=en)

61. What is a Partner?: Spotify & Genius make the perfect partnership (https://news.spotify.com/uk/2016/01/12/go-behind-the-lyrics-with-spotify-and-genius/)

62. What is a Partner?: Genius (https://genius.com/a/genius-and-spotify-together)

63. What is a Partner?: Virgin Trains and Festival No6 (https://www.virgintrains.co.uk/festivalnumber6)

64. Locating New Partners: ICE, held in London (http://www.icetotallygaming.com/)

65. Locating New Partners: Netflix (https://partner.netflix.com/en_us/)

66. Establishing whether a Partner is the right fit: Win an Aston Martin with PokerStars.com (https://www.pokerstars.com/en/blog/2006/pokerstars-and-aston-martin-racing-on-th-1-031486.shtml)

67. Establishing whether a Partner is the right fit: McDonalds and Monopoly (https://en.wikipedia.org/wiki/McDonald's_Monopoly)

68. *The Importance of Target Audience Similarity: GQ is an international monthly lifestyle magazine*
(https://en.wikipedia.org/wiki/GQ)

69. *The Importance of Target Audience Similarity: UK based Wilkinson Sword*
(https://en.wikipedia.org/wiki/Wilkinson_Sword)

70. *The Importance of Target Audience Similarity: GQ Magazine image from*
(http://www.gq-magazine.co.uk/promotions/wilkinson-sword/the-razor)

71. *The Importance of Brand Recognition & Reputation: Red Bull sponsorship is out of this world*
(http://www.redbullstratos.com/the-mission/world-record-jump/)

72. *Example of Audience and Brand Match: TripAdvisor and Deliveroo*
(http://www.bbc.co.uk/news/technology-40573272)

73. *Forging a Strong Relationship: E.ON is one Europe's largest electricity service providers*
(https://en.wikipedia.org/wiki/E.ON)

74. *Forging a Strong Relationship: Exclusive offering from EON and Tesco*
(http://pressreleases.eon-uk.com/blogs/eonukpressreleases/archive/2011/07/26/1727.aspx)

75. *Forging a Strong Relationship: Exclusive offering from EON and Tesco image from*
(http://www.seanmcpheat.com/wp-content/uploads/tesco-300x220.jpg)

76. *Following Brand Guidelines: Skype Brand Guidelines from*
(https://s-media-cache-ak0.pinimg.com/236x/f1/78/89/f17889490e0ecb826f156219573639ae.jpg)

77. *Establishing the Brand Positioning: Iceland and Disney's Frozen image from*
(http://www.disneymediaplus.co.uk/sites/default/files/styles/standard-media-image/public/case-study-videos/frozen%20video.jpg)

78. Integrated Partnerships: Starling Bank integrate round-up-investing App Moneybox
(https://www.starlingbank.com/blog/meet-moneybox-saving-investing/)

79. Integrated Partnerships: Citymapper & Uber
(https://citymapper.com/news/1276/best-of-both-worlds-uber-public-transit)

80. Pre-launch Testing: Guardian & Audible Partnership
(https://www.theguardian.com/gnm-press-office/the-guardian-audio-edition-launches-december-2012)

81. Pre-launch Testing: Guardian & Audible Partnership
(https://www.theguardian.com/gnm-press-office/the-guardian-audio-edition-launches-december-2012)

82. Pre-launch Testing: Guardian & Audible Partnership
(https://www.audible.co.uk/)

83. Utilising Social Media Techniques: Innocent Promote YesTo Partnership
(https://en.wikipedia.org/wiki/Innocent_Drinks)

84. Utilising Other Departments: BBC
(http://www.bbc.co.uk/news/technology-40573272)

85. Utilising Influencers: Sergio Aguero
(https://en.wikipedia.org/wiki/Sergio_Agüero)

86. Utilising Influencers: Puma
(https://en.wikipedia.org/wiki/Puma_SE)

87. Utilising Influencers: Sergio Aguero and Puma
(https://karllusbec.wordpress.com/2011/09/14/puma-signs-a-long-term-partnership-deal-with-aguero/)

DISCLAIMER & COPYRIGHT

information that will enable him to rectify any reference or credit line in subsequent editions. You hereby agree to be bound by this disclaimer.

<u>Copyright</u>

All images are referenced in the reference section of the book.
All company information has been taken from factual sources on the internet or from the authors personal experiences.

ABOUT THE AUTHOR

James Cristal has written this guide to Partnership Marketing from his own experience as a Senior Partnership Marketing Manager at FTSE 250 company Paysafe, one of the largest payment companies worldwide, and Growth & Partnership Manager at Nutmeg, the UK's largest wealth management robo-advisor.

James has created Partnership Marketing teams from scratch and acquired customers at record numbers. Over a five-year period at Paysafe he multiplied the affiliates and partnerships revenue tenfold. While at Nutmeg he doubled acquisition in the first year from 25k to 50k customers.

He has worked with hundreds of well-known brands from the likes of Moneysupermarket, RightMove, Financial Times, PokerStars, Skype, Bet365, and Samsung.

Through this experience he has honed his Partnership Marketing skills alongside digital marketing techniques for this evolving subject matter - all of which are featured in this book.

Acknowledgements

This publication has taken many hours of research, writing and editing, and the author wishes to express his gratitude to everyone who has assisted, namely Greg Cristal for inspiring him, and Nick Cristal, Ashley Cristal and Michele Miller for their ongoing encouragement. Special thanks goes to Debra Berkley, for all her help, this book is dedicated to her.

How to get in touch

James is also available for Partnership Marketing consulting, private tuition and training courses, so please do not hesitate to get in touch via LinkedIn or email if you are interested in his services:

jamcristal@hotmail.com
https://uk.linkedin.com/in/jamescristal

Printed in Poland
by Amazon Fulfillment
Poland Sp. z o.o., Wrocław